Striking Out

Striking Out
The Religious Journey of Teenage Boys

Donald Capps

 CASCADE *Books* • Eugene, Oregon

STRIKING OUT
The Religious Journey of Teenage Boys

Copyright © 2011 by Donald Capps. All rights reserved. Except for brief quotations in critical publications or reviews, no part of this book may be reproduced in any manner without prior written permission from the publisher. Write: Permissions, Wipf and Stock Publishers, 199 W. 8th Ave., Suite 3, Eugene, OR 97401.

Cascade Books
An Imprint of Wipf and Stock Publishers
199 W. 8th Ave., Suite 3
Eugene, OR 97401

www.wipfandstock.com

ISBN 13: 978-1-61097-300-7

Cataloging-in-Publication data:

Capps, Donald.

    Striking out : the religious journeys of teenage boys / Donald Capps.

    p. ; 23 cm. —Includes bibliographical references and index.

    1. Boys—Religious Life. 2. Teenage Boys—Religious Life. I. Title.

BV4450 C37 2011

Manufactured in the USA.

Credit: William Stafford, "Fifteen" from *The Way It Is: New and Selected Poems.* Copyright © 1966, 1998 by William Stafford and the Estate of William Stafford. Reprinted with the permission of Graywolf Press, Minneapolis, Minnesota, www.graywolfpress.org/.

Credit: Norman Rockwell, *Breaking Home Ties* printed by permission of the Norman Rockwell Family Agency Book Rights Copyright © 1954 The Norman Rockwell Family Entities.

[Scripture quotations are] from the New Revised Standard Version of the Bible, copyright © 1989 the National Council of the Churches of Christ in the USA . Used by permission. All rights reserved.

All scripture quotations, unless otherwise indicated, are taken from the HOLY BIBLE, NEW INTERNATIONAL VERSION®. NIV®. Copyright ©1973, 1978, 1984 by International Bible Society. Used by permission of Zondervan. All rights reserved.

Fifteen

South of the bridge on Seventeenth
I found back of the willows one summer
day a motorcycle with engine running
as it lay on its side, ticking over
slowly in the high grass. I was fifteen.

I admired all that pulsing gleam, the
shiny flanks, the demure headlights
fringed where it lay; I led it gently
to the road and stood with that
companion, ready and friendly. I was fifteen.

We could find the end of a road, meet
the sky on out Seventeenth. I thought about
hills and patting the handle got back a
confident opinion. On the bridge we indulged
a forward feeling, a tremble. I was fifteen.

Thinking, back farther in the grass I found
the owner, just coming to, where he had flipped
over the rail. He had blood on his hand, was pale—
I helped him walk to his machine. He ran his hand
over it, called me good man, roared away.

I stood there, fifteen.

—William Stafford

Contents

Acknowledgments / ix

Introduction / 1

1 The Stumbler / 12
2 The Struggler / 35
3 The Straggler / 66
4 The Straddler / 87
5 The Stranger / 116

Epilogue: Breaking Home Ties / 140

Bibliography / 145
Index / 147

Acknowledgments

I ESPECIALLY WANT TO THANK the editorial team at Wipf and Stock Publishers for their support along the way, especially K. C. Hanson, editor-in-chief, for his astute editorial observations and suggestions; also Jim Tedrick, managing editor; Christian Amondson, assistant managing editor; Diane Farley, editorial administrator; and Ian Creeger, typesetter. I would also like to express appreciation to James Stock, marketing director, and Raydeen Cuffe, marketing coordinator. My communications with Jeremy Funk, the copyeditor, have been especially welcome, as we came to know one another when he was a student at Princeton Theological Seminary. I knew from my reading of his student papers that the manuscript could not have been entrusted to a more perceptive copy editor.

The various communications I have had with the Wipf and Stock staff as my manuscript was being transformed into a book have reawakened memories of my own experiences in Oregon: first as a fifteen-year-old transplanted Nebraskan making my way through my high school and college years in Portland, then an all-too-brief stint as a thirty-year-old instructor in the Department of Religious Studies at Oregon State University before returning to the University of Chicago, where I had recently completed my doctoral studies.

When I was teenager, I would often hear people mention that so-and-so is "a journeyman." It was not said in a disparaging tone but I got the impression that the person was viewed as being rather ordinary. Later, I learned that it refers to a worker who has served an apprenticeship in a particular line of work and is an experienced, reliable worker who is not necessarily brilliant or likely to receive lavish praise. I found that I liked the word and over the course of my own life have personally identified with it. This book is written, therefore, in remembrance of the teenage boy who viewed himself as a journeyman and in recognition of the men and women of all walks of life who are members of this respectable cohort.

Introduction

DURING THE FIRST DECADE or so of life, the boy who grows up in a Christian home develops a familiarity with his religion. He goes to church with his parents, brothers, and sisters. He watches his parents participate in the church service and to the extent that he is willing and able to do so, he reads and sings along. If the minister presents a children's sermon, he joins the other children in the front of the church. He goes to classes that are modeled after their classes in school and learns about the Christian faith. When he visits his grandparents he may go to their church and take note of the fact that they do some things differently there. Or if the family moves to a different town or city, he notices differences between the new church and the old one. So he becomes aware that not all churches are the same, but, by and large, there is a certain familiarity with all of them—rows of pews, the minister up at the front, a choir off to the side, and so forth. Over time, he is likely to discover that there are some hymns he likes better than others. He may also like some stories from the Bible better than other stories. But these very preferences tend to reinforce, not undermine, his growing familiarity with his religion.

Things change at some indeterminate point in the second decade of life. The change is likely to be a gradual one, and because it is gradual, it may be imperceptible to him and to others. I believe that the word *journey* expresses what this change is all about. He begins to view himself as a person who is on a journey, and his religion begins to reflect this perception of himself. The externals of his religious engagements may look the same as he continues to go to church, to attend classes, and so forth, but something is changing inside of him. He is thinking about where his life is heading and his religion is implicated in these thoughts. As he enters high school and is given a chance to choose some of his classes, he begins to reflect more on what his interests are and to compare himself with other boys in this regard. It is a natural extension of these reflections to ponder where he is heading as far as his future employment is concerned.

As he moves into his junior year in high school, he begins (if he has not already done so) to reflect on the fact that he will need to make some plans for what he is going to do after he graduates from high school. He is likely to talk about these plans with other persons, such as a friend, a parent, a school counselor, or an older sibling. This is also the time when the question comes up of whether he is going to go to college and, if so, which one? For some boys the prospect of "going to college" does not mean "leaving home" because they assume that they will go to a local college and not live in the dorms. But for most boys these two go together. For them, the image of the *journey* is literally true. This is also true for those boys who plan to enter the armed services after graduation from high school, or who plan to work in a location other than their own city or town.

The very expectation that teenage boys will "leave home" soon after they graduate from high school is often reinforced by their parents' belief, whether directly stated or not, that this is the time when they *should* leave home. An assumption is deeply rooted in our culture that there is something wrong with a boy who does not want to leave home soon after he graduates from high school. Parents therefore anticipate their son's departure and may even plan their own lives around it. This is not to say that they necessarily want this to happen (though for some parents their son's departure does not come soon enough), and many parents know intuitively that they will feel bereft when their son leaves home. Much has been written about the "empty nest" phenomenon when a parent tries to come to terms emotionally with the fact that all of her or his children have left home. But even if there are younger siblings around and the nest is not empty, the departure of a son can be an emotionally difficult time for a parent. And yet, even these parents tend to feel that the time is right for the son to leave.

The *journey* motif is also often the theme of high school graduation ceremonies. The school principal or other invited speaker will typically employ this theme and will use it to invoke the values that the school has sought to instill in the students. Such speeches often conclude with good wishes for the graduates as they embark on their individual journeys.

There is nothing very remarkable, therefore, about the focus of this book on the religious journey of teenage boys. After all, if the boy is on a journey—and there is general agreement among all interested parties, including himself, that this is the case—then it makes perfect sense for us to view the religious dimension of his life in a similar way. In fact, an underlying assumption of this book is that there *should* be a congruity between the boy's life and his religion, so if he understands himself to be on a journey we would want him to think of this journey as, in part, a *religious* journey. But this means that, as far as his religion is concerned, there is likely to be much that is subject to change because his life is changing. It also means that these changes in his religion would reflect his effort to come to terms with the challenges that he experiences and confronts as he ventures out and continues on his journey. In other words, the changes in his religion would serve a good purpose.

Some of these changes will necessarily involve doubts relating to the boy's earlier religious formation. However, as Gordon W. Allport points out in *The Individual and His Religion*, not all doubts are the same. Some doubts are primarily reactive and negativistic while other doubts are associated with the genesis of the religious quest. The latter are a reflection of the fact that the boy is growing and maturing and that his religion is a reflection of this growth and maturation.[1]

Since I will be using the image of the *journey* throughout this book, it is important for us to have a clear idea of what the word means. According to *Webster's New World College Dictionary*, it has two basic meanings: (1) the act or an instance of traveling from one place to another; and (2) any course or passage from one stage or experience to another.[2] What is noteworthy about both definitions is the assumption that one is not only leaving a place or stage but also intending to reach another place or stage. One is headed toward a destination and not merely wandering about or going in circles.

The dictionary indicates that the word *journey* is a derivative of the Latin word *diurnum*, which means "a daily portion." So originally *journey* implied the distance that one could travel in one day. The word *journal*, which is also a derivative of the Latin word *diurnum*, originally

---

1. Allport, *The Individual and His Religion*, 103–10.
2. Agnes, ed., *Webster's New World*, 773.

meant a daily record of happenings, such as a diary.[3] However, in time *journey* came to mean an act or instance of traveling of an indeterminate duration. It could be a day, but it could also be several days, weeks, months, or even years.

Once its duration became indeterminate, the word *journey* could be used as a metaphor, to refer, for example, to a mental, psychological or spiritual process, or to a person's whole life from birth to death. Yet, the idea that the journey has a destination has been retained, and this means that we think of a journey as being intentional and purposeful. One is going *somewhere*. This also means that journey is understood to be forward-looking. One may occasionally take a glance back to see how far one has traveled, but the basic idea is that one is oriented toward the future, not the past or even the present. In fact, when we think of a person being on a journey, we are inclined to think that being oriented to the present is no better than being oriented to the past. And this is what makes the image of the journey so relevant to the teenage boy, because for the teenage boy the future is clearly predominant in a way that it was not when he was in the first decade of his life. Everyone who is thinking of his best interests—including teachers, parents, other adults, and even his friends—are encouraging him to think about where he is going and to plan ahead. Vocational counselors will sometimes ask a high school boy, "Where do you expect to be in five years?" When the boy answers, the counselor may say, "Then let's think about what you need to do to get there."

Another interesting thing about the image of the journey is that it can apply to a single individual who is traveling all alone, but it can also apply to a group of individuals who are traveling together. Take, for example, Jesus's Parable of the Good Samaritan (Luke 10:25–37). One of the reasons why the man who was traveling from Jerusalem to Jericho was vulnerable to robbers was that he was traveling alone. If he had been among a group of travelers, it's doubtful that the robbers would have been able to strip him, beat him, and leave him half-dead. In fact, a single companion traveler may have been enough to dissuade the robbers from attacking him.

Because high school graduation is a time when most teenage boys are thinking about leaving home, there is very much the sense that one is embarking on a journey in the company of others. To be sure, each boy tends to have his own plans for the future and this means that the

3. Ibid.

journeyers are not bound for the same destination. Some are heading toward college, and although they are not planning to attend the same college, they nonetheless share in common the anticipation that for the next four years they will be taking classes, making new acquaintances, making career choices, and so forth. Others are heading toward military service and are anticipating that they will go through a rigorous training process with other recruits and quite possibly discover that the military is the right career for them, or that it has provided training and experience that will be helpful in another profession or occupation. Still others are planning to enter the labor force immediately upon graduation from high school and begin their move up the organizational ladder. Whatever their destination may be, they are very much aware of the fact that others are setting out on the same journey, and that they will necessarily encounter these others as they continue on their journey.

On the other hand, the teenage years are ones in which boys are likely to become aware of the fact that they are individuals. Of course, they always knew this. After all, throughout grade school the fact that each boy is an individual was emphasized in many different ways: if a teacher called on one boy and another boy answered in his stead, he would be reprimanded for speaking out of turn. The issue was not merely that the teacher was interested in eliciting the right answer, but that she wanted to know if the boy she had called on knew the right answer. Also, as a teacher became familiar with her class, she learned about the abilities and liabilities of each of the students, and took their individuality into account as she related to them. Sometimes, of course, she would treat them as a group ("All right, class, line up"). But more often than not, she would place their individuality ahead of their membership in the group.

So the fact that a teenage boy is an individual is nothing really new. But in the teenage years there is a growing, deepening sense of oneself as a person. In *The Varieties of Religious Experience*, William James says that a crab would probably be filled with a sense of personal outrage if it could hear us class it as a crustacean. If it could speak, it would say, "I am no such thing. I am myself, myself alone."[4] Teenage boys can identify with the crab because they are experiencing a growing awareness that "I am myself." Many, too, can identify with the crab's added emphasis, "myself alone," because their growing sense of being an individual is ac-

4. James, *The Varieties of Religious Experience*, 9.

companied by a growing sense of aloneness despite the fact that they are members of a group.

I want to suggest here that this sense of being "myself, myself alone" is what makes the journey a religious one. As Allport writes in the concluding section of *The Individual and His Religion*, titled "The Solitary Way": "From its early beginnings to the end of the road the religious quest of the individual is solitary. Though he is socially interdependent with others in a thousand ways, yet no one else is able to provide him with the faith he evolves, nor prescribe for him his pact with the cosmos."[5]

What makes Allport's use of the word "quest" significant is that it implies that the *religious* journey, or that aspect of the boy's journey that is *religious* in nature, is not a simple matter of getting to a predetermined destination. The dictionary defines *quest* as a journey in search or pursuit of something, typically a lofty or noble goal.[6] Thus, it is precisely the *religious* aspect of the boy's journey that introduces an element of uncertainty into what might otherwise be a simple, clearly defined journey from this point to that point. In addition, although the boy is "socially interdependent with others in a thousand ways," the *religious* aspect of his journey is personal, so much so that it is experienced as "the solitary way."

Thus, the religious journey is the most personal and therefore solitary. But it is also the most self-encompassing, for "the religious sentiment" is "the portion of personality that arises at the core of the life and is directed toward the infinite," the "region of mental life that has the longest-range intentions, and for this reason is capable of conferring marked integration upon personality, engendering meaning and peace in the face of the tragedy and confusion of life." So the very fact that the religious sentiment *is* that portion of the boy's personality that "arises at the core of the life and is directed toward the infinite" makes the word *quest* an appropriate one, for, as noted, *quest* implies a search or pursuit of a lofty or noble goal. Much more is involved here than the more immediate questions with which the teenage boy is confronted in his junior year in high school, such as where to go to college, which unit of the armed services to join, whether to seek employment in his home city or town or to go to some other city or town, and so forth. As Allport concludes, "A man's religion is the audacious bid he makes to

---

5. Allport, *The Individual and His Religion*, 141–42.
6. Agnes, ed., *Webster's New World*, 1176.

bind himself to creation and to the Creator" and "is his ultimate attempt to enlarge and to complete his personality by finding the supreme context in which he rightly belongs."[7] This is itself rather lofty talk. But the religious sentiment cannot settle for less, and because it cannot settle for less, it is necessarily vulnerable to misjudgments, misunderstandings, and mistakes. This very fact brings me to the primary focus of this book.

The title and subtitle of this book together are *Striking Out: The Religious Journey of Teenage Boys*. I use the phrase *striking out* in two senses. The dictionary defines *striking out* as "to begin, advance, or proceed, especially in a new way or direction."[8] This definition is especially relevant to the teenage boy because he is just beginning his journey from home, and he and others know that he will be proceeding or advancing in a new way or direction. But *striking out* has another meaning, one that is associated with the game of baseball. As the dictionary puts it, this is "an out by a batter charged with three strikes."[9] This definition has a strong implication of failure, for an out due to being charged with three strikes is worse than an out where the batter at least hits the ball but the ball is caught, or he is thrown out at first base. Although the outcome may be the same—an out is an out—there is a difference between walking back to the dugout after being called out on strikes and running to first base after hitting the ball. The first is much more humiliating. Also, there is always the chance that the batter who connects with the ball advances another runner so the out is not necessarily a total failure. In fact, if the runner was on third base, the batter who connects with the ball may well produce a run, perhaps even the game-winning run. In which case, he is a hero. Not so the boy who is called out on strikes. He and his teammates know that his at-bat was a total failure.

But this is a book about the *religious* journey of the teenage boy, and this puts a very different spin on the second definition of *striking out*. A humiliating experience in the eyes of a boy's teammates may not be so in the eyes of his Creator. His Creator may, in fact, notice how he walks back to the dugout after striking out and may say to himself, "I like the way that boy carries himself. He has failed miserably. But there is something about the way he responds to his failure that I myself can appreciate." Of course, there is a danger involved in thinking that we know

7. Ibid.
8. Agnes, ed., *Webster's New World*, 1418.
9. Ibid., 1419.

what the Creator is thinking, of assuming, for example, that the Creator prefers a boy who does not hurl invectives at the umpire or throw his bat down on the ground in disgust, but who instead holds his head high as the adults in the stands and his coach and teammates in the dugout let him know that they are displeased with his performance. Still, it makes good sense to assume that the Creator who considers the larger picture views a boy's failure in a very different way from that of the persons, including the boy himself, who cannot see the larger picture.

The first definition of *striking out* focuses on the fact that the teenage boy is embarking on a journey. And, as I have been suggesting, the fact that it has a *religious* aspect means that it is a journey that is more, not less, vulnerable to misjudgments, misunderstandings, and mistakes. To make this vulnerability more concrete, I will focus on five manifestations of this vulnerability. Since the religious sentiment is that portion of the boy's personality that is most solitary, on the one hand, and long-ranging and integrative on the other hand, I will use words that personalize these five manifestations of the boy's vulnerability. They are the *stumbler, struggler, straggler, straddler,* and *stranger*. The following are brief descriptions based on dictionary definitions:

(1) *Stumbler*: one who trips or misses his step on walking or running, or walks in an unsteady or awkward manner; one who speaks, acts, or proceeds in a confused, blundering manner; one who falls into sin or error; and one who discovers something by chance, as in stumbling onto an important clue or insight.[10] The *stumbler* is relevant to teenage boys because some boys often, and other boys occasionally, have a tendency to be awkward (both physically and socially); to be vulnerable to confusion, resulting in being ridiculed or treated with disdain by other teenagers; and to make moral mistakes that may have profound consequences.

(2) *Struggler*: one who makes his way with great difficulty, often exerting great effort or a series of attempts before giving up.[11] The *struggler* is relevant to teenage boys because some boys often, and others occasionally, will try to accomplish things that they have not tried before, such as dating, attempting to excel in athletics, music, mountaineering, driving a car, working in a part-time job, doing volunteer work, figuring out what he wants to do with his life, and the like. He often learns the hard way what he can do well and what he is unlikely to master no matter how hard he tries.

10. Ibid., 1422–23.
11. Ibid., 1421.

(3) *Straggler*: one who strays from the path or course, or wanders from the main group; one who falls behind the others.[12] The *straggler* is relevant to teenage boys because some boys often, and other boys occasionally, find it difficult to keep up with the others, whether scholastically, socially, or physically. Unlike the *stumbler,* theirs is not so much a case of being awkward, confused, or susceptible to falling, but rather a case of moving along at a slower pace due, in part, to slower maturation or to being interested in things that are not of central interest to the majority of teenagers.

(4) *Straddler*: one who takes or appears to take both sides of an issue or refuses to commit himself to one side or the other; also, there is a physiological connotation to the word *straddle,* that of placing oneself with a leg on either side of a chair, bench, pole, or other object.[13] The *straddler* is relevant to teenage boys because some boys often, and others occasionally, are unsure of what they think or believe and therefore remain noncommittal, doing so at a time when other boys are taking a firm or even a strong stand on a given issue or claim. If they do take a stand, they may do so with such intensity that they know they are trying to convince themselves that this is right or true, or to impress adults or other teenagers with their sense of conviction.

(5) *Stranger*: an outsider, newcomer, or foreigner; a person not known or familiar to one; a person who is unaccustomed to some particular or specified thing.[14] The *stranger* is relevant to teenage boys because some boys often, and other boys occasionally, experience themselves as strangers to other teenagers, parents, and adults in light of changes that are occurring in their self-perceptions, their perspectives on the world, and so forth. They may also experience themselves as strangers to themselves, for there may be new aspects or features of their personalities that they themselves do not understand, that seem foreign or alien to them. They ask themselves, "What, or perhaps more accurately, *who* has gotten into me?"

I would suggest that the first three—the *stumbler, struggler,* and *straggler*—form a trio because they portray the boy as having difficulty moving forward on the journey and staying up with the others. He may therefore be feeling rather isolated and alone on the journey. On the

12. Ibid, 1414.
13. Ibid.
14. Ibid., 1415.

other hand, each of these three may have other companions who are *stumblers, strugglers,* or *stragglers,* and he and these others may join together and perhaps make something of a virtue out of the very fact that they are having difficulty keeping up with the larger group or choosing not to even try to keep up with it. How they join together and make a virtue of their vulnerability is important to explore because this can have positive and/or negative implications and consequences.

I would also suggest that the two remaining ones—the *straddler* and *stranger*—form a pair because they focus on the boy's internal sense of being somewhat or very much at odds with himself; that is, as being unable to speak with a common voice or act with a singleness of intention or purpose. The *straddler* may be unsure of what he thinks or believes, or may have come to believe, at least tentatively, what he is not supposed to believe. The problem here is largely mental or intellectual, but it may have important emotional determinants or consequences too. The *stranger* is likely to be more concerned with emotions and feelings that are unfamiliar and, because they are so, they may be disturbing or threatening. This can have mental consequences, for he may think that a boy like himself should not feel this way. As noted earlier, he may wonder what—or who—has gotten into him, and adults and other teenagers who have known him may wonder this too. With both of these—the *straddler* and the *stranger*—there is the very real prospect of self-condemnation, and however justified he may feel in condemning himself, the goal of personal integration will suffer as a result.

On the other hand, it is important to recognize that these five manifestations of a boy's vulnerability are not necessarily negative (or wholly so). The dictionary has a positive meaning of the *stumbler,* namely, one who discovers something by chance, as in stumbling onto an important clue or insight. Similarly, the *struggler* may learn through his struggles that some things with which he struggles are integral to the person he is and wants to become, while others are not. As for the *straggler,* he may find that his distraction from what others consider important is something well worth noticing and finding out more about. The others may fail to notice it because they are too concerned to move along and maintain their pace. Perhaps if they were less concerned to keep moving, they would take notice of it too.

The *straddler* and *stranger* may also have positive meanings. For example, the *straddler* may find that some issues are more complex than he or others realize, and that it is wise to straddle these issues rather than to try to settle them prematurely. Thus, his inability to take a position or express certainty about an issue may be an indication of his growth toward a more integrated person. Similarly, the *stranger* may find that there is something about the new emergent emotions and feelings that he is experiencing that he can welcome; they may, in fact, be aspects of his personality that he had dismissed or rejected earlier but that have returned and are seeking recognition and endorsement.

As we explore these five vulnerabilities in the following chapters, I will be illustrating them with examples from the lives of teenage boys. It is important to keep in mind, however, that these are merely illustrations of the vulnerability in question. We should not assume that a boy who experiences one or another of these vulnerabilities is necessarily defined by this vulnerability. After all, a particular boy may have had a relatively brief period during his teenage years when he experienced himself as a *stumbler*, a *struggler*, a *straggler*, a *straddler*, or a *stranger*. It may, in fact, have been so fleeting that others (adults and other teenagers) failed to notice it, or if they did notice it, did not attach much significance to it. He may have felt the same way and viewed the experience as quite insignificant. On the other hand, the experience may have had enormous significance for him and have played an important role in his religious journey.

My point here is that I am not trying to typecast individual boys and to assign them to a particular category even if they see themselves in this light. Rather, I am suggesting that these are common experiences of teenage boys as they strike out on their religious journey, and that these categories help us to understand and appreciate how a boy's religious sentiment influences the development of his personality. As we have seen, the religious sentiment is "the region of mental life that has the longest-range intentions, and for this reason is capable of conferring marked integration upon personality, engendering meaning and peace in the face of the tragedy and confusion of life."[15] I am suggesting that a teenage boy's experiences of being a *stumbler, struggler, straggler, straddler,* and *stranger* are central to the development of these longest-range intentions. The following chapters will, I hope, provide compelling evidence in support of this suggestion.

---

15. Allport, *The Individual and His Religion*, 142.

1
The Stumbler

As we saw in the introduction, there are several ways a teenage boy may be a *stumbler*. One is to trip or miss his step in walking or running, or to walk in an unsteady or awkward manner. A second is to speak, act, or proceed in a confused, blundering manner. A third is to fall into sin or error. A fourth is to discover something by chance, for example, to stumble onto an important clue or insight. In this chapter we will meet teenage boys who have these experiences of stumbling.

A Father's Advice to His Teenage Son

To set the stage for these accounts, and to underscore the fact that we are concerned here with the *religious* journey of teenage boys, I suggest that we consider a biblical text that relates to the theme of stumbling. The book of Proverbs is especially appropriate because much of it is presented as a father's advice to his maturing son. It is easy to imagine that these words of fatherly advice were spoken to the son as he was leaving home, for in the first chapter, the father says, "Hear, my son, your father's instruction, and reject not your mother's teaching" (1:8). Then he introduces the journey metaphor and tells his son not to consent to the enticement of thieves who ambush passersby and steal their goods. The father says, "My son, do not walk in the way with them, hold back your foot from their paths" (1:15).

Once he has introduced the metaphor of the journey, the father introduces the image of stumbling. He tells his son to "keep sound wisdom and discretion" and not to let them escape from his sight for "then you will walk on your way securely and your foot will not stumble" (3:21–23). Later, the father asks (or pleads with?) his son to hear his instructions and to "be attentive, that you may gain insight" (4:1), and says that he is telling his son these things so that "the years of your life may be many," for "I have taught you the way of wisdom. I have led you in the paths of uprightness. When you walk your step will not be hampered; and if you run, you will not stumble" (4:10–12).

He issues another word of caution against walking in the way of evil men, men who cannot go to sleep at night "unless they have made someone stumble" (4:16), then observes that it is not all that difficult to distinguish the path of righteousness from the path of wickedness because the path of righteousness "is like the light of dawn, which shines brighter and brighter until full day" while the way of the wicked "is like deep darkness; they do not know over what they stumble" (4:18–19). Of course, one can stumble during the day when it is light, but one is far more likely to stumble at night when it is dark.

The father concludes these instructions to his son—who is about to strike out on his own—by advising him:

> Let your eyes look directly forward,
>   and your gaze be straight before you.
> Take heed to the path of your feet,
>   then all your ways will be sure.
> Do not swerve to the right or to the left;
>   turn your foot away from evil. (4:25–26)

The implication is that evil lurks in the bushes alongside the pathway, for this is where those who are up to no good hide and ambush those who are journeying from home to their intended destination. These evil men will be attempting to entice him, a young man just starting out, to join them; so if he keeps his eyes on the pathway ahead he will not see them and they will not be able to catch his gaze. This also implies that the eyes have a direct effect on the feet—if the eyes turn one way or the other, the feet are likely to turn as well, and stumbling may result.

Much of what the father has to say here is cautionary, especially in its emphasis on avoiding the evil men whom the son is likely to encounter as he leaves home and strikes out on his journey. But the words also include a strong note of promise, namely, that if the son follows his father's advice, the years of his life will be many. As we know from the genealogies in the Bible (for example, Gen 5:3–32 and 11:10–32), a very high premium was placed on living a long life. In effect, a long life was a sign of God's favor. But there was also the belief that a long life has intrinsic value because it enables one to do more good. For example, "A good man leaves an inheritance to his children's children" (Prov 13:22). There is much greater likelihood of his doing this if he is actually around to witness the birth of his children's children. But this is just one of the many ways in which a longer life affords more opportunities to do good things for others.

As we have seen, the father's instructions focus a great deal on avoiding the evil men who are lurking in the bushes. Later, however, there is a proverb that makes this observation:

> He who walks with wise men becomes wise,
>   but the companion of fools will suffer harm. (13:20)

Here the focus is not on the men who are lurking in the bushes but on one's traveling companions. These may be persons with whom one begins the journey, or persons whom one meets along the way who, unlike the men lurking in the bushes, are also on a journey. The message here is that one will be better off if one chooses wise rather than foolish traveling companions A sign that one has chosen wise companions is that one becomes wiser oneself. Conversely, a sign that one has chosen foolish companions is that one suffers harm to oneself. The father here seems to know from his own personal experience what he is talking about. After all, appearances can be deceiving, and one may not be able to tell which companions are wise and which are foolish until one has traveled a reasonable distance in their respective company.

Finally, a father's instructions to his son who is just striking out on his journey would not be complete if it did not say something about the Creator. As we saw in the introduction, the religious quest, from its beginnings to the end of the road, is a solitary one. On the other hand, "a man's religion is the audacious bid he makes to bind himself to creation and to the Creator."[1] The father in the book of Proverbs has this to say:

> A man's mind plans his way,
>   but the LORD directs his steps. (16:9)

This way of viewing the relationship between the traveler and the Lord may be a bit surprising, for teenagers are often advised to seek

---

1. Allport, *The Individual and His Religion*, 141–42.

God's plan for their lives and then to follow it to the best of their ability. The proverb suggests almost the opposite: use your own mind to plan your way—in other words, decide on your destination—and once this has been decided, the Lord will direct your steps. The way you go is up to you and your best judgment, and the Lord's role is to direct your steps, how you put one foot forward, then another and another.

This may appear to be a rather minor role for the Lord to play. But it actually underscores the importance of the stumbling motif: The Lord knows that stumbling is always a real possibility but is there to help you *not* to stumble and fall. Another proverb suggests that the Lord is very much involved in the destination as well:

> Many are the plans in the mind of a man,
>   but it is the purpose of the LORD that will be established. (19:21)

Although this proverb may appear to contradict the previous one, this is not necessarily the case, for this proverb focuses on the fact that a person may be mulling over many different and perhaps irreconcilable plans, so the fact that one can rely on the Lord to arrest all of this mental confusion and resolve it in favor of his own purposes can come as a very welcome relief. This, however, is not the same situation as when a person strikes out on a journey toward a certain destination but encounters some rough spots along the way that may cause him to trip or miss his step—the situation, in other words, that concerns us here. For this situation, just knowing that the Lord will be there to direct his steps, and thus to minimize the number of missteps and their resulting harm, can be enormously reassuring. This is especially the case for a teenage boy who knows that the journey is long and the destination itself is uncertain.

Saint Augustine: Stumbling into Sin and Error

If the advice of a father to his son in the Proverbs warrants our attention, we can also learn a lot about stumbling from the very first Christian autobiography, the *Confessions* of Saint Augustine. In fact, if the father in Proverbs warns his son to avoid the company of thieves, Augustine tells us about what happened to him when he and some boys engaged in an act of theft. In the second chapter of his autobiography he tells about an episode that occurred in his sixteenth year, which he spent in idleness waiting to begin his studies at Carthage where he would take a course of studies intended to prepare him for a career in law.² His family home was in Thagaste (in northern Africa), but he had been going to school in the nearby town of Madauros, where he studied literature and oratory. But his studies there were interrupted because his father wanted to send him to Carthage instead. So he was called home and spent several months in idleness. This hiatus saved money that would otherwise have been spent on his education in Madauros and also provided time for his father to raise the necessary funds for him to attend the university in Carthage (which was about 275 miles from Thagaste). Augustine notes:

> At the time everyone was full of praise for my father because he spent money on his son beyond the means of his estate, when that was necessary to finance an education entailing a long journey. Many citizens of far greater wealth did nothing of the kind for their children. But this same father did not care what character before you I was developing, or how chaste I was so long as I possessed a cultured tongue—though my culture really meant a desert uncultivated by you, God. You are the one true and good lord of your land, which is my heart.³

He tells two stories about what happened during his year of idleness. The first was when he and his father were in the bathhouse and his father "saw that I was showing signs of virility and the stirrings of adolescence," and was "overjoyed to suppose that he would soon be having grandchildren, and told my mother so."⁴ His mother did not share his father's enthusiasm in this regard. He says, in fact, "she feared the twisted paths along which walk those who turn their backs and not their face towards you."⁵ Notice his use of the image of the journey to convey his mother's fear that his sexual development would lead to trouble. What kind of trouble? "Her concern (and in the secret of my conscience I recall the memory of her admonition delivered with vehement anxiety) was that I should not fall into fornication, and above all that I should not commit adultery with someone else's wife."⁶

He confesses that these warnings "seemed to me womanish advice which I would have blushed to take the least notice of," but they were in

---

2. Augustine, *Confessions*, 24–34.
3. Ibid., 26.
4. Ibid., 26–27.
5. Ibid., 27.
6. Ibid.

fact God's own warnings: "I believed you were silent and that it was only she who was speaking, when you were speaking to me through her."[7] Not realizing this,

> I went on my way headlong with such blindness that among my peer group I was ashamed not to be equally guilty when I heard them boasting of their sexual exploits. Their pride was the more aggressive, the more debauched their acts were; they derived pleasure not merely from the lust of the act but also from the admiration it evoked. What is more worthy of censure than vice? Yet I went deeper into vice to avoid being despised, and when there was no act by admitting to which I could rival my depraved companions, I used to pretend I had done things I had not done at all, so that my innocence should not lead my companions to scorn my lack of courage, and lest my chastity be taken as a mark of inferiority.[8]

The other story is his account of his involvement in the stealing of a huge load of pears from a neighbor's orchard. There was a pear tree near his parents' vineyard that was filled with fruit, and he, together with some other boys, had been playing games in the street. As it got dark, they could not play anymore but did not want to return to their homes. So they decided to steal the pears. It wasn't a matter of needing the fruit. In fact, he had plenty of the fruit already from his parents' orchard, and it was much better quality than the pears he stole. His desire "was to enjoy not what I sought by stealing but merely the excitement of thieving and the doing of what was wrong."[9] Indeed, after he and his comrades carried off the fruit, they threw the bulk of it to the pigs. To be sure, they may have eaten a few of them, but their pleasure lay in doing what was not allowed.

Looking back, Augustine considers the possibility that some people may take the kinds of liberties he and his friends took that night because they perceive that God is above the law, and they think that this kind of behavior may have "a shadowy likeness" to the freedom that God himself enjoys. Augustine intimates that he may well have thought this at the time of the theft. But if so, he soon realized that there is no pleasure to

---

7. Ibid.
8. Ibid., 27–28.
9. Ibid, 29.

be gained from such an act of "deformed liberty," for what he had done was unlawful, and there's no pleasure to be gained from unlawful acts.

He also considers the likelihood that he had noticed "a poverty of justice" and "a glut of evil-doing" in Thagaste, so what he did could perhaps be viewed as a sort of protest. If the adult world that he was about to be joining was full of corruption, the pear theft—which, after all, pales in significance to the wrongs committed by adults—might be viewed as a symbolic gesture, however perverse, of protest. Looking back, Augustine does not find this argument very convincing, and doesn't think that it gets to the heart of why he did what he did.

So why did he do it? If he had gotten something of value from the theft, he would at least have a clear rationale for why he did it. But this was not the case at all. After all, if he wanted pears, there were better ones in his parents' own orchard. And, in any case, they had thrown the bulk of the pears out for the pigs to eat. So there had to be a better explanation, and a key to this explanation is that he is certain he would not have done it if he had been alone. But this very fact raises the question, why was the fact that he did it in company with the other boys the critical factor? Was it because it's more fun to do something wrong when one is in a group than when one is doing it alone? He recalls that he and the other boys laughed a lot after they had done the deed. And while it is possible for a person to be overcome with laughter when no one else is around if something very funny affects the senses or strikes the mind, there is something rather special about laughing as a group. So the fun of doing something wrong together with other boys was certainly a factor in why he did something that he would not have done alone.

But does this fully explain why he participated in the theft? No. In fact, a more compelling reason for why he did it was that he was shamed into doing it. Prior to the theft, he had heard the other boys boast of their disgraceful acts, and the worse they were, the more they boasted. So that he would not be scorned, he had made up stories about his own misdeeds so that he would be on equal footing with the others. So when someone in the group said, "Let us go and do it!" he had the feeling of being "ashamed not to be shameless." In effect, he did not want to appear weak or cowardly.

Does his claim that he would not have done it if it weren't for the others mean that he is trying to rationalize his involvement in the theft, to shift the blame onto the others? I think not. He concludes his reflections on the experience with this remorseful observation: "As an adolescent I went astray from you, my God, far from your unmoved stability," and "I became to myself a region of destitution."[10] He had stumbled and fallen, and he had only himself to blame for this, for he knew that stealing was wrong and that nothing good could come from it. If he did not want to appear weak and cowardly to the other boys, was this really worth the loss of his very source of stability? No, it was not. And the irony was that in his desire not to be shamed in the eyes of the other boys, he is now deeply ashamed of himself—shamed, as it were, in his own eyes.

Augustine's stumbling experience happened centuries ago, but it has a lot of elements that are quite contemporary. It begins, for example, with the question of where he should get his education—at a school nearby or a school with a much better reputation that is "a long journey" from home. His parents are necessarily involved in this decision because they will be footing the bill. As we have seen, his father very much wants his son to go to the school with the better reputation. Augustine believes that this was largely because his father wanted to impress the other parents in town, that he was not really concerned about his son's own best interests. It also appears that his father was heavily involved in the decision as to what his son would become. As Augustine puts it, "My studies which were deemed respectable had the objective of leading me to distinction as an advocate in the law courts, where one's reputation is high in proportion to one's success in deceiving people."[11]

Needless to say, there are many people today who share Augustine's view of lawyers. But he implies that this was considered a respectable profession in those days. It is quite conceivable that Augustine was asked by other travelers on the long journey to Carthage what he would be studying to become, and that they were quite impressed when he responded that he was going to study to become a lawyer. And although, in retrospect, he feels that he was headed in the wrong direction, it is entirely conceivable that he did not feel that way at the time. In fact, he may have answered the other travelers' question with much the same sense of personal satisfaction as a teenage boy today who is heading off to Harvard with the ultimate intention of being admitted one day into Harvard Law School.

10. Ibid., 34.
11. Ibid., 38.

On the other hand, is there not a certain incongruity between the fact that Augustine would soon be heading off to study law in Carthage and the fact that he had taken part in the theft of a load of pears from a neighbor's orchard? A high school counselor today might be prompted to agree with Augustine that the theft was a sort of protest, but that it was not only—or primarily—a protest against the corruption he had witnessed in the behavior of the adults in his home town but a protest against the plan that he would go off to Carthage to study law. What better way to protest against this plan than to engage in an unlawful act? In fact, it is not inconceivable that he felt, perhaps unconsciously, that by engaging in an unlawful act he would effectively sabotage the plan for him to become a lawyer.

Of course, from his retrospective view as an adult in his early forties who did not become a lawyer after all, he could reconcile his engagement in the theft with the fact that lawyers are judged on the basis of how good they are at deceiving others. However, I doubt that this was the view of lawyers that his father had when he was engaged in acquiring the funds needed to send his son to the University at Carthage. So if his parents found out about the theft and their son's engagement in it, perhaps they simply considered it an insignificant moral lapse and nothing more. Or perhaps his father was so preoccupied with acquiring the funds to send his son to the best school that money could afford, that he didn't pay any attention to what his son was doing or feeling at the time. All we really know is that Augustine blames his father later for seeming not to care about what was going on inside his son but was instead only thinking of the externals: a well-educated son with a promising and perhaps lucrative career as a lawyer.

Although Augustine mostly blames his father, he is also critical of his mother. As he says of his parents: "Both of them, as I realized, were very ambitious for me: my father because he hardly gave a thought to you [meaning God] at all, and his ambitions for me were concerned with mere vanities; my mother because she thought it would do no harm and would be a help to set me on the way towards you, if I studied the traditional pattern of a literary education. That at least is my conjecture as I try to recall the characters of my parents."[12] He also notes that although his mother did not share his father's enthusiasm over the prospect of grandchildren, this was apparently not because she was opposed to his

12. Ibid., 28.

engaging in sexual behavior on moral grounds, but because a wife could impede his career prospects, and she did not want this to happen. Thus, she encouraged him to guard his virginity, but if he could not restrain his sexual urges, she wanted him to stay away from married women (which could lead to legal entanglements?). So, in effect, his parents' ambitions for him clouded their judgment, and despite the fact that they were well intentioned, they, along with his friends, contributed to the fact that his long journey to Carthage was an ill-fated one. It was not that the destination in this case was unclear or unknown. It was that the destination itself was wrong for him.

Jim: The Boy Who Stole

An attractive woman in her late thirties or early forties called the pastor of a Protestant church in the small rural community where she lives with her husband, Ed, and three teenagers.[13] Jim, the oldest, is seventeen years old. Her daughters are fifteen and thirteen. When Mary called, she asked the minister (whose given name was Jeremiah, but who was Jerry to church members and friends) if he would be in his office if she stopped by, and he said that he would. Jerry knew all the members of the family casually because they lived in his immediate neighborhood but had not had any personal contacts with any of them. They were members of the Roman Catholic church in town. Ed was a skilled carpenter who provided well for his family, although he had a reputation for drinking heavily. When Mary arrived at the church, Jerry welcomed her into his office, and she began to state her problem without any preliminaries.

She said that she wanted to ask him what might be the best thing to do about her son Jim. She and her husband, Ed, were at the end of their rope and needed to get some help because "Jim's in trouble again." She asked Jerry if he had heard about it, and he said he hadn't. So she proceeded to tell him that Jim, who was working after school in one of the town's grocery stores, had been caught taking money from the cash register. He had admitted to the owner and his parents that this was not the first time he had taken money from the cash register.

Mary was especially troubled by the fact that "Jim isn't sorry for what he has done. I just can't understand it." She explained that Mr. Moore, the grocery store owner, who was a member of Jerry's own con-

13. Cryer and Vayhinger, *Casebook in Pastoral Counseling*, 162–66.

gregation, had been "so kind to Jim and us. He isn't going to do anything about it—go to the law, I mean. He said he'd take Jim back on the job, if we say so—but I can't feel sure that Jim wouldn't do it again."[14]

Jerry responded that he was sorry to hear about this and believed he knows how she feels and would like to help in any way that he can: "But are you sure that I am the person you want to talk to? Wouldn't Father Ambrose be the one to help you with this?" Mary responded, "I can't go to him. He's down on Jim already. He wouldn't help. Jim wouldn't talk to him anyway. They kicked him out of school last semester—said the sisters couldn't handle him—and Jim hasn't gone to Mass since." Jerry recalled that Jim was now enrolled in the public high school, although the two daughters attended the parochial school. When Jerry replied that he was very sorry to hear this, Mary broke down and cried:

> I'm just sick—ashamed and hurt. We tried so hard to raise the kids right. We've really tried. I feel so—so helpless! We've failed, somehow. I don't know how, or why, but we've failed our son, some way. This business at the grocery store is just about more than I can take. When they dropped Jim from school I told Father Ambrose that it was the Sisters' fault if Jim got in trouble in school. I told him that he was a good boy at home, and never gave us any trouble. But he does, of course. I just didn't want to admit it to the priest.[15]

Jerry said that we all have our shortcomings and none of us likes to admit them. Mary brightened up a bit and replied, "That's just what I told Ed. There aren't any perfect parents, I said, but some of them are luckier than others." She added, however, that Ed thought differently: "He thinks this is a judgment on us. But I don't believe that Jim is the devil's disciple." Puzzled about the "devil's disciple" phrase, Jerry asked her what she meant by it, and she explained, "Well, that's what Father Ambrose said—he couldn't help Jim as long as he was in league with the devil. Ed says he won't make Jim go and see Father Ambrose."[16]

To Jerry's question about whether Ed has any ideas about helping Jim, Mary simply replied, "Oh, he agrees that something has to be done. Jim is our only son—we can't let him grow up to be a thief." Jerry then asked how Jim gets along with his father, and Mary responded:

14. Ibid., 163.
15. Ibid.
16. Ibid.

Pretty good—at least I always thought so. Oh, they have their arguments, but Ed tries to help him, too. In the summers he takes Jim with him on the job—and brags on him. Says he is good help. Jim likes that, naturally. He likes to think he's important, you know—helping to build houses. And then, he gets Jim things he wants—like that leather jacket last month. Jim didn't need it at all, but he wanted it, and his dad got it for him. Sometimes I think he gets too much. That's why I can't understand why he should get into this kind of trouble. It isn't as if he didn't have any spending money and everything else he needs. Actually, he gets more than most boys his age.[17]

Jerry said to Mary that this is "a very perplexing situation," then added that it sometimes takes a great deal of time and effort "to get to the bottom of problems like this so that one can understand why children behave in such a fashion."[18] He then asked her if she had thought about consulting a family agency where they have caseworkers especially trained to help parents work out problems like this. When she said that she hadn't thought of this, he suggested that she might consult the public child welfare agency and gave her information about making an appointment with the agency. He also gave her his card because they will probably ask her who referred her to the agency. Two weeks later he received a form letter from the agency indicating that Mary and Ed had made an application for service from the agency.

In his written comments on this conversation with Mary, Jerry said that it was fortunate that a public agency with highly skilled personnel was available because there were few if any other viable alternatives. In other communities it might be practical to consult with the parish priest, but in this particular community this would have done more harm than good. Furthermore, Mary had come to him for help because she felt she could not go to the priest.[19]

In his comments on this case, Paul B. Maves, who was a seminary professor of religious education at the time, observed: "There is more here than meets the eye. Stealing is only one piece of evidence of maladjustment. We have little data that can provide clues to the meaning of these acts or indicate the approach that should be taken. There is a hint of a family pattern of maladjustment. The community may be at

17. Ibid., 163–64.
18. Ibid., 164.
19. Ibid., 164–65.

fault in not providing its youth with sufficient opportunities for recreation, vocational training, or economic advancement. And there may be other problems."[20]

He added that this seems to be a situation where the employer should not forgive and forget: "The boy needs to recognize the gravity of the offense and make restitution, to re-establish his integrity." Furthermore, he is in need of counseling "to work through his own attitudes."[21]

What is especially interesting about this case is that Jim has begun to stumble and fall, and no one seems to know quite why. Or, perhaps more accurately, they have a number of theories as to why, but no one of these theories is conclusive. In fact, some of them contradict others.

Mary thinks that she and Ed somehow failed as parents but doesn't know how or why. She suggests that Ed has been too indulgent toward Jim and gives him too much, but if so, Jim's need to steal doesn't make much sense because it isn't as if he doesn't have any spending money. In fact, he actually gets more than most boys his age.

Father Ambrose thinks that the devil has gotten his hands on Jim, and if Mary's representation of his views is accurate, he doesn't think there is anything he can do as long as the devil has control of Jim.

Pastor Jerry does not have a theory about why Jim has begun to stumble and fall, but this is because he thinks that there is something deeper going on, and that time and effort will be required to get to the bottom of it; until that occurs, no one will know for sure why Jim has begun to stumble and fall.

Professor Maves suggests that there is a hint of a family pattern of maladjustment, and that the community may not be providing its youth with sufficient opportunities for recreation, vocational training, or economic advancement.

We, the readers of this illustration, may also be able to come up with other plausible explanations or at least to arrive at some judgments as to which of the ones that have been presented already are the most persuasive. It may help in this regard if we view the cases of Augustine and Jim together. After all, they share in common the fact that neither of them really needs whatever it is they have stolen. Augustine already has access to better fruit, and as Mary points out, it isn't as if Jim doesn't

20. Ibid., 166.
21. Ibid.

have enough spending money. Perhaps, then, the community issue that Maves raises is especially critical. After all, Augustine indicates that he and the other boys did not have enough to keep them occupied in their small town, so they stole the pears out of a need for some excitement. On the other hand, he confesses that this was not a sufficient explanation for why he, personally, got involved in the theft. This, in fact, may be where the two cases begin to part company, for Augustine believes that the best explanation for his behavior was that he did not want the other boys to think that he was weak or cowardly or not as bad as he had pretended to be. In contrast, Jim was stealing from the cash register on his own, without any apparent encouragement from other friends.

On the other hand, there may be a more important connection between the two cases. We noted that there was an incongruity between Augustine's unlawful act and the future that had been planned for him, which was to take the long journey to Carthage to study to become a lawyer. Could it be that Jim, who will soon be graduating from high school, is also looking down the road and, for whatever reason, does not like—or fears—what he sees? And might it be that his stealing from the cash register is also a protest against this future? Mary says, "Jim is our only son—we can't let him grow up to be a thief." This is perfectly understandable. But perhaps the very fact that he *is* their only son and that they could never allow him to become a thief (as if to say that if they had several other sons they might be able to tolerate one of them turning out badly as this would reflect more on him than on them) indicates that, as in Augustine's case, they are very ambitious for their son. It would not be at all surprising if these ambitions were becoming a burden to him, especially at a time when he is beginning to strike out on his own. And perhaps the fact that he is reluctantly carrying this burden—or defiantly resisting it—makes him more vulnerable than he would otherwise be to stumbling on the rocks, roots, and debris on the path in front of him.

In any event, we ourselves would seem to be on the right track if we were to look toward the foreseeable future for an explanation for why Jim is stealing from Mr. Moore's cash register. That is, we would not focus, as the others are doing, on the past or even the present. This would mean that the various explanations for his behavior that they have offered are not necessarily wrong but are somewhat beside the point. Even if they are right, will they help Jim to walk more sure-footedly on the path that lies before him? I rather doubt it. This seems to be where Augustine comes out too. Having looked at the pear theft episode from all sorts of angles he concludes that he is unable to untie this "twisted and intricate mass of knots" and does not "wish to think about it" anymore. He simply wants to get back on the path from which he has strayed.

Supposing, then, that a stranger came to the small rural community where Jim lives with his family and learned through the grapevine that Jim had been stealing from Mr. Moore's cash register and had been expelled from the parochial school because the sisters couldn't handle him. And supposing this stranger contrived to bump into Jim at, say, the local McDonald's where Jim would sometimes go for a burger, fries, and coke. How might this stranger come to Jim's assistance? He might make a mental note of the fact that although Jim is still living at home, he has already embarked on what is, in fact, a *religious* journey. Father Ambrose may have understood this fact better than anyone else. But if so, what good does it do to suggest that Jim is "in league with the devil"?

The stranger might, instead, mention a poem by John Henry Newman, written in 1833 that was later set to music. At the time he wrote the poem, Newman was not a Roman Catholic. His conversion occurred a decade later. But he had been traveling in Sicily and had been stricken with typhoid fever and nearly died there. On his return trip when he was somewhere out at sea, he wrote a poem titled "The Pillar of the Cloud," a reference to the cloud by which the people of Israel were guided during their wilderness wanderings (Num 9:15–23). This poem is better known as "Lead, Kindly Light," the words with which it begins. No doubt the hymn has been popular over the years because people resonate with the idea that the light is *kindly*. Some lines of the poem would not be relevant to Jim's situation, but these most certainly are:

> Keep thou my feet; I do not ask to see
> The distant scene; one step enough for me.[22]

Would Jim appreciate these words? Who knows? But he may be more likely to appreciate them when they come from the lips of a traveler who has stopped for a meal in Jim's hometown and does not profess to know what the others know or assume that they know. How could he even presume to understand (as Jerry expressed it) "why children behave in such a fashion" when he doesn't really know the "child"? And

---

22. Newman, *Verses on Various Occasions*, 156–57.

how could he presume to understand that this is a case of family maladjustment or of a community that does not provide its youth enough of what they need, or of the devil having gone about the community and having made disciples of vulnerable teenage boys? After all, he is a stranger, and all that he knows is that Jim has been getting into trouble at school, at home, and at the grocery store where he works after school.

What he also knows, however, is that when Jim was expelled from parochial school and ceased attending Mass, he embarked on a very solitary religious journey not unlike the one that John Henry Newman embarked upon when he left his traveling companions in Rome and set off for Sicily for reasons that were as unclear to him as they were to his companions. Where this solitary journey will take Jim is not for him to know or presume to know. What he *does* know, however, is that Jim will be less likely to stumble if he relies on the kindly light that keeps his feet, one step at a time.

As the stranger gets up to leave, should he suggest to Jim that he ought to make restitution to Mr. Moore? Although Augustine does not claim to have done so, this would save Jim's parents from having to provide Mr. Moore their own assurances that he will not steal again if he goes back to work at the grocery store. I think, rather, that he should leave this to Jim to decide on his own. He has done his work, and it is time for him to go. For as the poem notes, the night is dark, and he is far from home.

Hessu: Discharge without Mercy

Ben Furman was doing his residency in a psychiatric hospital in Helsinki, Finland, when he came into contact with Hessu, an eighteen-year-old boy who had been hospitalized for having slashed his wrists after a bout of heavy drinking.[23] He had a personal history of many difficulties and disappointments. Due to his parents' severe alcohol problems, he had been taken into custody at an early age by child welfare workers; they placed him, along with his younger brother, in a children's home. He had experienced many problems himself on his way to adulthood, but recently, as he approached the coming of age, he had begun to study to make up for missed classes at school. He had also become interested in

---

23. Furman and Ahola, *Solution Talk*, 21–23.

getting his high school diploma, which was essential for entering any vocational school.

On the hospital ward Hessu appeared to be a determined young man who really intended to regain control of his life. The special teacher at the hospital reported that he had begun helping Hessu with his studies. Hessu was also doing his chores and was getting support from his girlfriend, who was studying with him. Contact was made with his social worker at the department of child welfare, and arrangements for where he would live after his hospital treatment was over were being made.

Everything seemed to be going well when one evening, after he had been in the hospital for only three weeks, Hessu came back from one of his evening leaves in a severely drunken state. There were strict regulations against patients' use of alcohol. Intoxication during treatment meant the discontinuance of treatment and discharge from the hospital. Since Ben was in charge of Hessu's treatment he announced to the staff on the ward that he would have to be discharged. Then he personally informed Hessu about the decision. With a look of appeal on his face Hessu asked to be allowed to stay. But Ben held onto his judgment, believing it to be entirely fair. As he explained to Hessu, "You know that we all like you and we would be happy to keep you here. However, if I do not discharge you that would mean that I think you are weak, that you wouldn't make it. I believe that despite what you have been through in your life, you are a strong person. Therefore you will have to leave."[24] Hessu appeared to understand Ben's point, and he accepted the verdict.

Then, however, Ben received a phone call from the special teacher at the hospital, who emphasized to Ben how he had successfully worked with Hessu during the past weeks, and how Hessu had made remarkable progress. He pleaded with Ben to call off the discharge. The next day Ben received a telephone call from Hessu's social worker from the department of child welfare, who told him about the many hardships in Hessu's life, and about how hard she and her colleagues had worked over the years to help him become able to stand on his own feet. She worried that now that there was finally some real progress, discharge could be a setback that Hessu would not be able to cope with.

Ben realized that he was in a difficult position. To give in to the pleadings of the teacher and the social worker would have meant taking back his words about his belief in Hessu's strength and that he will be

24. Ibid., 22.

able to make it despite the fact that he will be leaving before his hospital treatment had been completed. So he decided to assemble a meeting with everyone with an interest in Hessu. In addition to Hessu, there was the child welfare worker, the teacher, and several staff members. Everyone was given an opportunity to speak, and this meant that Hessu was able to hear what they had to say about him. But after they had spoken, Ben indicated that he was going to stand by his decision because to refrain from discharging Hessu for his violation of the intoxication regulation would indicate that they did not believe he had to strength to make it in the world outside the confines of the hospital. For this reason, the only possible course of action was to proceed with the discharge.

Hessu left after a few days. Ben did not hear anything about Hessu until some years later when he met the social worker who was now working as an alcohol counselor. She informed Ben that after Hessu had been discharged he had been placed temporarily in a guesthouse where his room was paid for by the department of child welfare. She noted that despite her initial apprehensions, Hessu began to take increasing responsibility for his life after the discharge and was both attending vocational training and employed in a job related to his vocational training.[25]

Hessu stumbled the night he returned from an evening leave in a drunken state. We can well imagine that he, quite literally, manifested these visible signs of stumbling: walking in an unsteady or awkward manner and speaking, acting or proceeding in a confused, blundering manner. In any event, his intoxication was evident to the staff members who were on duty that night. But more important than these visible signs was the fact that he had fallen. Some would say that he had fallen into sin. Others might say that the word *sin* is too strong a word and not very helpful. But all would agree that he had committed a serious error. After all, he had jeopardized his treatment program and had done so just at the time that those who were working with him were noticing how well he was doing. He was doing so well, in fact, that plans were being made about where he would live after his hospital treatment was over.

What is noteworthy here is that neither he nor Ben Furman questioned the validity of the strict regulations against intoxication during treatment. Nor, in fact, did any other person involved. Their disagreements had to do with whether the circumstances in this case would justify making Hessu an exception to the rule. And what would be the

25. Ibid., 23.

grounds for treating Hessu as an exception? That he had been making impressive progress toward the goal of regaining control of his life. Why allow this single act of stumbling to play such an influential role in his journey toward an ultimately productive life? The others were asking Ben to show some mercy based on Hessu's recent performance.

The dictionary defines *mercy* as a refraining from punishing an offender and as a kindness in excess of what may be expected or demanded by fairness.[26] No one, including Hessu himself, seemed to view his discharge as unfair. If strict regulations against intoxication were not already in place and Ben had made a unilateral decision that Hessu's behavior warranted discharge, then the charge of unfairness would certainly have been an appropriate one. But no one was suggesting that Ben was treating Hessu unfairly. They simply wanted him to consider the fact that Hessu was making excellent progress toward the goal of regaining control of his life and their belief that his progress might not continue if he were discharged before his treatment had been completed.

As we have seen, Ben did not take their advice and show mercy to Hessu. As he points out, he felt that if he had done so he would, in effect, have been taking back his words about his belief in Hessu's strength. It was important, however, that he arranged for everyone to meet, including Hessu himself, so that he could hear the arguments that were being made in support of his *not* being discharged. An interesting thing about these arguments is that they actually supported Ben's view that Hessu was strong enough to make it on his own. The special teacher had noted how Hessu had made remarkable progress, and the child welfare worker had also noted that Hessu was finally making progress toward being able to stand on his own feet.

Another interesting thing about these arguments is that they represented Hessu as being on a journey and as making progress toward a destination. If we think of this illustration in light of John Bunyan's classic *The Pilgrim's Progress*,[27] we might give a name to this destination; for Bunyan tells of how Christian traveled from the City of Destruction to the Celestial City and encountered various towns, structures, valleys, and forests along the way—all of them having names that identified the challenges they presented or the resources they provided. We might, for example, suggest that the first destination in Hessu's journey was the

---

26. Agnes, ed., *Webster's New World*, 901.
27. Bunyan, *The Pilgrim's Progress*.

city of Self-Reliance—reflecting the title of a well-known essay by Ralph Waldo Emerson.[28] As Emerson makes clear in this essay, self-reliance does not mean that we do not need to rely on others. (In *The Pilgrim's Progress*, Faithful accompanies Christian on the first half of his journey and Hopeful accompanies him on the second half.) It simply means availing ourselves of the strengths that we possess and not losing heart when our initial efforts miscarry, for "with the exercise of self-trust, new powers shall appear"; and, furthermore, "a man who stands on his feet is stronger than a man who stands on his head." [29]

Ben believed that Hessu had the strength to make it in the city of self-reliance, and he also believed that his telling Hessu so would add to Hessu's own confidence that he could make it there. The fact that he had stumbled and fallen was not to be minimized. But it was not, in Ben's eyes, a sign that he lacked the strength to make it on his own.

In his account of Christian's pilgrimage, Bunyan tells of how Christian, having left the City of Destruction where he was born and raised, and having traveled through the Slough of Despond and Morality Village, came to Interpreter's House. Through object lessons and enacted parables, Mr. Interpreter teaches Christian what he will need to know for his journey. He introduces Christian to two small children, Passion and Patience, who are staying at Mr. Interpreter's house. Passion is very discontented because he wants everything now; Patience, however, is willing to wait for the better things to come. Christian learns from this living parable that Patience has the "best wisdom," because the things close at hand are ephemeral and the things for which he waits are substantial and enduring. Christian is also introduced to a man in an iron cage who cannot repent of his sins. This terrible sight prompts Christian to pray that God will help him to watch and be sober and to shun the sins that are the cause of the caged man's misery.

With various lessons and parables of this nature, Mr. Interpreter provides Christian his schooling in the Christian faith. He introduces him to the dangers and opportunities that lie ahead, but more important, he teaches him the method of interpretation itself, as he guides Christian in his efforts to understand the meaning of the object lessons and parables presented to him. The method of interpreting life's situa-

---

28. Emerson, "Self-Reliance."
29. Ibid., 275, 282.

tions becomes an invaluable resource as Christian later confronts situations whose meaning is not self-evident.

The meeting of all the persons involved that Ben assembled may be viewed in a similar light. All were given the opportunity to present their interpretation of the effect that Hessu's violation of the regulations and mandated discharge would have on his progress toward regaining control of his life. In effect, Hessu was introduced to the method of interpretation itself. Interpretations are not the same as explanations. No one seemed all that interested in explaining why Hessu got drunk that evening. No doubt they had previously covered the ground of his alcohol abuse and its relation to the fact that his parents were both alcoholics, and were not inclined to go through all of that again. What interested them was what was likely to happen to Hessu once he left their care, and this became a matter not of idle speculation but of informed interpretation based on what they knew about him and about the challenges that he would be confronting as he left the hospital and embarked on his largely solitary journey. How would he get along? This was the crucial question, and there was no way to answer this question in advance of the journey itself.

We do not know what happened during the brief period after his discharge that Hessu spent in the guesthouse where his room was paid for by the child welfare department. I would like to think, however, that this was a time in which he reflected on what had happened in the hospital. In Bunyan's terms, the hospital could have functioned as Morality Village, emphasizing his violation of the strict regulations for intoxication. Instead, by Ben's refusing to treat Hessu as an exception to the rule and also by his assembling the persons involved for a discussion of the possible impact of his early discharge from the hospital, the hospital became a contemporary version of the Interpreter's House. So as Hessu struck out toward the city of Self-Reliance he carried with him an invaluable resource that he may not have acquired had he not stumbled and fallen where there were others to witness his fall and to help him regain his footing.

Bert: Authorization

In one way or another, the illustrations presented above cover the three primary dictionary meanings of the *stumbler*, as one who trips or misses his step in walking or running, or walks in an unsteady or awkward manner; one who speaks, acts, or proceeds in a confused, blundering manner; and one who falls into sin or error. In light of the fact that we are especially concerned with the *religious* journey, or that aspect of a boy's journey that expresses his "ultimate attempt to enlarge and to complete his own personality by finding the supreme context in which he rightly belongs,"[30] it was perhaps inevitable that the third form of stumbling would have an especially prominent role in these illustrations. And, of course, they focus on only a small number of the ways that teenage boys may fall into sin or error. Now, however, it is time to consider the fourth meaning of the *stumbler* as one who discovers something by chance, as in stumbling onto an important clue or insight.

To illustrate this meaning, we will consider the story of Bert, a nineteen-year-old boy who had left his family home in Phoenix, Arizona, to go to college in Ann Arbor, Michigan.[31] He wrote to his father and said that he wanted to buy a car and added that he needed his father to sign the documents that would permit him to drive the car because he was a minor. His father wrote back, telling him that he couldn't sign the authorization because he couldn't assume the responsibility: "I'm in Arizona," he said, "and you're in Michigan." Then he added, "Surely you can find some businessman with a good reputation who will sign it for you."[32]

Bert didn't know any businessmen with a good reputation, so he went down to the police department in Ann Arbor and entered the office of the police chief, who was sitting at his desk. He told the police chief that he was only nineteen years old and wanted to buy a car, but that his father lived in Arizona and didn't feel he could sign the authorization papers that would allow him to drive it: "I'd like to have you sign it for me." The chief was startled by this request, and asked him if he was out of his mind. Bert said that he was perfectly sane and asked him to at least think it over. The chief thought for a moment then said, "Give me that paper," and he signed it.[33]

Bert was well aware of the fact that the man who was taking responsibility for authorizing him to drive a car was the same man who had the power to take away this authorization if Bert did anything that violated his right to drive the car. Furthermore, this man would know

---

30. Allport, *The Individual and His Religion*, 142.
31. Rosen, *My Voice Will Go with You*, 216–17.
32. Ibid., 216.
33. Ibid.

if he had done so because, after all, he would have ready access to any reports that Bert had committed a driving or parking violation.

Bert had recently left home and was striking out on his own. His initial hope was that he could turn to his father for help in this particular instance, but his father was reluctant to assume the responsibility. He suggested, however, that Bert should be able to find a businessman with a good reputation to sign for him. This was a reasonable suggestion, but where would Bert find such a person and would he be willing to vouch for a young man whom he did not know? How could he be sure that Bert was a responsible boy? So Bert stumbled onto an alternative plan that was designed to reduce or even eliminate the signer's risk.

In his comments on this illustration, Sidney Rosen suggests that the message in this story may be that one need not fear authority, that one can, in fact, "engage or utilize authority in the fulfillment of one's goals."[34] He adds that the authority in this case was responsive to an effective approach, an approach that was effective, in part, because it was rather unorthodox, and for this very reason commanded attention. We assume that these messages were not lost on Bert himself, and as a result he has stumbled onto some important insights about authority that will be enormously helpful as he continues on his journey. It seems appropriate too that this illustration has to do with the question of how he will get from here to there. Although his purchase of a car means that he will not be getting there on foot, we can be confident that he will do his best to avoid the automotive equivalents of the other three forms of stumbling—for example, running red lights, driving while intoxicated, or exceeding the speed limit.

---

34. Ibid., 217.

2
The Struggler

As WE SAW IN the introduction, the *struggler* is one who makes his way with great difficulty, often exerting great effort or a series of attempts before giving up. I noted that this experience is relevant to teenage boys because this is a period in life when a boy will try to accomplish things he has not done or attempted before, such as dating; trying to excel in athletics, music, or mountaineering; driving a car; trying to figure out what he wants to do with his life; and so forth. He often learns the hard way what he can do well and what he is unlikely to master no matter how hard he tries. Through his struggles, he is likely to learn that some things with which he struggles are integral to the person he is and wants to become while other things are not. Thus, struggling may be an intrinsic aspect of gaining insight into his identity and what he hopes to become in his life.

I also suggested that the *stumbler, struggler,* and *straggler* make a trio because they express the fact that the boy is having difficulty progressing on the journey on which he has embarked and is having problems of one sort or another in staying up with the others. He may therefore be feeling rather isolated and alone on the journey. He may also be feeling some resentment over the fact that the others do not seem to be experiencing the difficulties that he is experiencing, that they seem to be able to take everything in stride. Finally, though, I suggested that the *stumbler, struggler,* and *straggler* may have companions who are also *stumblers, strugglers,* or *stragglers* and that he and these others may join together and perhaps make something of a virtue out of the very fact that they are having difficulty keeping up with the larger group or choosing not to even try to keep up with it.

The *struggler's* tendency to fall behind may be simpler and more straightforward than is the case with the other two. It is likely that he genuinely wants to keep up with the others and, unlike the other two, is avoiding distractions, deceptive companions, and the like. But he simply lacks the stamina to keep pace with the others. Lack of stamina can mean various things in this context: that he has not been adequately prepared for the journey, that he lacks the inner and external resources for a journey that entails some difficult challenges, or that he perceives that the others do not especially value his company. We will be exploring these and other reasons for the *struggler's* difficulties in the course of this chapter.

As we do so, it may be useful to point out at the outset that there is a general tendency in our society to admire the *struggler*. In fact, we often make invidious comparisons between the *struggler* and the other four vulnerabilities. We tend to think that the *stumbler* could have been more careful, the *straggler* lacks incentive, the *straddler* lacks conviction, and the *stranger* poses a threat. In contrast, the *struggler* evokes our admiration because he refuses to give up or accept defeat but instead keeps trying no matter how tempting it may be to quit, take a rest, or turn back.

My purpose in raising this issue is not to question our instinctive admiration for the struggler. But this very admiration can add to the difficulties the struggler experiences, because it may cause him to struggle on against his own better judgment. He may, for example, feel that his struggling isn't getting him anywhere, that he is misusing his energy—energy that could be redirected toward an objective more germane to the person that he is and seeks to become. This can be and often is a religious issue because, as Gordon Allport points out, our religious sentiment is "the region of mental life that has the longest-range intentions and for this reason is capable of conferring marked integration upon personality."[1] Sometimes, the very fact that an objective is a matter of considerable struggle is due to the fact that this objective is incongruent with one's longest-range intentions and therefore causes one to feel divided, at odds with oneself. So, we can admire the *struggler* because he refuses to quit or to give up, but we also need to keep in mind that

---

1. Allport, *The Individual and His Religion*, 142.

struggling isn't everything, and there are times when the ability to give up or abandon the struggle deserves our admiration too.

Saint Augustine: Struggling in Carthage

In the previous chapter we focused on an experience in Saint Augustine's life in which he stumbled and fell. He was sixteen years old at the time. We also noted that his stumbling may have been connected to his resistance to his parents' ambitions for him, and especially his father's desire that he would go to the university at Carthage and study to become a lawyer. In the next chapter of his autobiography, he tells about his experiences in Carthage. As we will see, these were years in which he was essentially the *struggler*.[2]

His life as a student in Carthage began auspiciously. He soon rose to the top of the class in the school of rhetoric, and he was very pleased with himself, even to the point of becoming rather conceited. But he was far quieter than the other students. Also, he did not engage in the vandalism perpetrated by the gang of students who called themselves "the Wreckers." To be sure, he kept company with them and sometimes delighted in their friendship, but he was appalled by their behavior. They would persecute the entering freshmen by mocking their tendency to be quiet and shy, and their hesitancy to speak in class. Augustine does not explain in detail how the Wreckers mocked the freshmen, but says that they perverted the younger students' modesty and seduced them into becoming mockers themselves.

Noting that he himself was "at a vulnerable age," he knew, of course, that his task was to study the textbooks on rhetoric. He had a strong desire to distinguish himself as an orator. One of the assigned texts was Cicero's *Hortensius,* which was written near the end of Cicero's life. Its main purpose was to challenge Hortensius's view that philosophical study has no social value and does not contribute to human happiness. Cicero relied on Aristotle's argument that only someone with a philosophical mind is able to judge the validity of Hortensius's claim, so this proves the value of philosophical study. The book had a tremendous influence on Augustine. He writes: "The book changed my feelings. It altered my prayers, Lord, to be towards you yourself. It gave me different

---

2. Augustine, *Confessions,* 35–51.

values and priorities. Suddenly every vain hope became empty to me, and I longed for the immortality of wisdom with an incredible ardor in my heart."[3] Augustine says that he did not read the book "for a sharpening of my style, which was what I was buying with my mother's financial support now that I was eighteen years old and my father had been dead for two years."[4] He was impressed not by its effect on his style and literary expression but by its content.

Specifically, it created in him a love of wisdom. He recognizes that there are some people who use philosophy to lead others astray, often by giving their way of doing philosophy a name and then claiming that it is the true philosophy. But this is why Cicero's book was so helpful to him, for Cicero challenged these philosophers' claims and advised his readers not to study one particular philosophical school but to love, seek, pursue, hold fast, and strongly embrace wisdom itself, wherever wisdom is to be found.

Augustine felt, however, that there was one major omission in Cicero's inspiring book. This was the fact that he made no reference to Jesus Christ. He had ingested the very name of Jesus Christ with his mother's milk "and at a deep level I retained the memory." Any book that lacked this name, however well written or polished or true, could not entirely grip him. So he "decided to give attention to the Holy Scriptures in order to find out what they were like."[5] This was a good idea in principle, but when he began to read the Bible, he felt that it was unworthy in comparison with the dignity of Cicero's work. In retrospect, he knows that the Bible is a text of "mountainous difficulty and enveloped in mysteries." At the time, though, it seemed humble and not very well written. He now understands that his inflated view of his own intelligence prohibited him from appreciating the Bible's "restraint," and that his "gaze never penetrated its inwardness."[6]

This reaction explains why he fell in with the Manicheans, who claimed to be authentic Christians, but who in Augustine's later judgment, were more talk than substance. He says that they would "sound off" about God to him "frequently and repeatedly with mere assertions

---

3. Ibid., 39.
4. Ibid.
5. Ibid., 40.
6. Ibid.

and with the support of many huge tomes."[7] But what they gave him was pictures of food to assuage his hunger, not the food itself. So where was God in relation to himself? Unfortunately, God was very distant. If only he had followed the intelligence of the mind that God had given him, he would not have been taken in by the Manicheans.

His mother was troubled by the fact that he had fallen in with the Manicheans, and had evidently decided that she would no longer fund his education. So he took lodgings at the home of a wealthy Manichean who helped with the cost of his education. She also had a dream in which she was standing at one end of a wooden measuring rod and a young man, who was handsome, cheerful and smiling, came to her and asked her why she was so downcast. She told him that she was mourning the fact that her son had gone astray. He told her not to worry and to look at where she was standing. She looked and saw her son standing beside her. When she related her dream to Augustine, he interpreted its meaning to suggest that she had moved to where he was, not that he had moved to where she was. Given the dream's inherent ambiguity, his interpretation seemed very plausible. But she vehemently disagreed and said that the word spoken to her was not "Where he is, you will be also," but "Where you are, there he will be also."[8] In the end, her interpretation proved to be the correct one, but it was nine years before he joined her on her end of the measuring rod.

She also consulted a bishop who was brought up in the church and asked him to talk with her son and to refute the errors and false doctrines he had embraced and teach him good ones instead. The bishop refused her request on the grounds that Augustine was not ready to learn the truth because he was still wrapped up in the novel excitements of these heretical teachings. Moreover, it was clear from what she had told him that her son had already upset many untrained minds with "trivial questions." The bishop added that *his* mother had gotten him involved with the Manichee sect when he was a small boy, and that he had not only read nearly all their books but had even copied them. In time, he was able to see for himself that the sect should be avoided, and he didn't need anyone to provide a refutation of their teachings. But she was unwilling to take no for an answer, and continued to plead with him to talk with her son. At this point he got irritated with her and told her to leave, add-

7. Ibid., 41.
8. Ibid., 50.

ing his assurance that it is simply impossible that the son of such tears should perish. When she related this conversation to Augustine, she said that she embraced these words as if they had "sounded from heaven."[9]

Most of Augustine's account of his student years in Carthage centers on his academic life and his decision to become a member of the Manichean religious organization. But there were sexual struggles as well. The year he arrived in Carthage he became involved with a Carthaginian woman of low social status. He notes that he met this woman in church and confesses that he lusted after her during the service. He attributes his overtures to her to his penchant for acting the role of a man who had a lot going for him. She returned his affections, and over the next several years he says that he was punished for their love affair with feelings of jealousy, suspicion, fear, anger, and contention. They had a son ("unwanted") who was named Adeodatus, and the three of them lived together for fifteen years until he became engaged to an upper-class girl whom he did not marry because his conversion to the orthodox Christian faith intervened.

Related to his sexual struggles was his love of the theater. He attributes this love to the fact that the shows he went to were full of representations of his own miseries. Mostly, they were miseries relating to his love life: "I shared the joy of lovers when they wickedly found delight in each other," and when "they lost each other I shared their sadness by a feeling of compassion."[10]

That Augustine was struggling at this time in his life is very evident from the way he describes his student years in Carthage. His father had died, and his death probably meant that Augustine was at least formally released from his father's desire that he would become a lawyer. Yet he was taking the courses and reading the books that would prepare him to become a lawyer, for the primary qualification to be a lawyer was that he was trained in rhetoric. After all, he needed to be persuasive in court. He was the top student in his class, but one senses from his comment that he was quieter than the other students that his grades were based on his written work. It is entirely possible that he felt for the entering freshmen who were quiet and reticent because he identified with them. He was appalled, therefore, that the mockery of the Wreckers turned these quiet and reticent students into loudmouths like themselves.

9. Ibid., 51.
10. Ibid., 36.

Cicero's book became Augustine's salvation because it spoke to him in a very personal way. In effect, it said in words what he was feeling inside. But Cicero was not a Christian, and the Manichees claimed to be Christians, so, in his hunger for fellowship, he became a member of their organization. The fact that one of its members provided financial support for his education is an indication of the fact that he was not only struggling to find the truth but also struggling with the very practical implications of the fact that his father was deceased and his mother was supporting his education.

There was also the fact that when Augustine went to the Bible, he found it a great disappointment. He does not tell readers what he read in the Bible, but his later observations that he failed to appreciate its "inwardness," together with the fact that he was deeply impressed with Cicero's appeal to wisdom, may indicate that he did not get very deeply, if at all, into the Wisdom literature (which he quotes extensively in his autobiography). Nor, apparently, did he take notice of the fact that Jesus, the very one whose name was missing from Cicero's book, was a teacher and practitioner of wisdom (as reflected in his proverbs and parables, and in the ways in which he engaged in quiet conversations and healed the sick).

If this was a period of struggling, what, in fact, was Augustine struggling for? What was it that he wanted or sought, but that remained so elusive? The simple answer is that he was seeking God. But the more complex answer is that he was seeking happiness. As he notes in the concluding chapter of his autobiography, "when I seek for you, my God, my quest is for the happy life."[11] The difficulty he experiences in this quest is that he is not sure how he or anyone else came by the idea of happiness in the first place. Do they remember having felt happy at some earlier period in their life? If so, how did they know to call it happiness instead of something else? One thing seems clear, and this is that everyone wants it. No one would give a negative response to the question, do you want happiness? On the other hand, there is not much, if any, agreement among us as to what makes for happiness. If two persons are asked if they want to serve in the army, one may say yes and the other may say no, but both may be responding on the basis of what makes them happy. Finally, however, because he has never met a person who wanted to be deceived, Augustine believes he can safely affirm that the happy life is

11. Ibid., 196.

joy grounded in truth, and this means that the quest for happiness is the quest for God.

It may be that Augustine was unaware of what he was struggling for when he began his student years at Carthage. If someone had asked him if he was struggling to find happiness, he may have agreed with a rather perfunctory "Well, isn't that what everyone wants?" But it is unlikely that he would have given the issue much thought. On the other hand, the experience of reading Cicero's book seems to have been one that created the very sense that he *could* be happy. In other words, it kindled in him the hope of happiness, and as he points out in an earlier chapter, some people are happy in hope of becoming so. It also created in him a hunger for the truth. So, in a very real sense, the book inspired him to think of happiness and truth as being one and the same.[12]

Then, however, he began to flounder. The Bible was a disappointment and the Manichees were not reliable guides on the road to truth and happiness. There was also the fact that he was in a committed relationship that was not, however, leading toward lawful marriage. In short, he was struggling, and it was to take a decade or more for him to gain clarity as to which things were worth struggling for, and which were not (the difference being that the former were integral to the person he aspired to be).[13]

Michael: Life Is Hard

Michael is seventeen years old and lives in a suburb in a city in the Midwest. He is one of more than one hundred boys whom William S.

---

12. In *Mood and Personality* Alden E. Wessman and David F. Ricks present the case of a university student they refer to as a "happy man" (145–73). They note the following: "A steadfast optimism, supported by independence and an active orientation toward the world, sociability and love of human contact, and a balance and maturity of judgment were apparent in Winn's life history, daily behavior, test productions, and mood dynamics . . . While various other men we studied certainly surpassed him in complexity and richness of personality, in depth and extent of awareness and creative potentialities, in dedication to particular goals or in other valued characteristics, none equaled Winn in genuine happiness" (167, 169). They cite in this connection Aristotle's view that happy individuals tend to possess "the element of durability" required in view of the changes to which one is subject in the course of life (169).

13. Chapters 4–8 of the *Confessions* offer a personal account of his struggles in the next stage of his life, and Part 2 of Peter Brown's work, *Augustine of Hippo: A Biography*, provides an excellent account of these years of continued struggle.

Pollack, a clinical psychologist at Harvard Medical School and McLean Hospital (a psychiatric hospital in Somerville, Massachusetts), interviewed in the late 1990s.[14] Michael begins his reflections on his current situation with the comment, "Life is hard," then adds, "I really don't know where to start. I guess I'll start with school. It already takes up about eight hours of each of my weekdays." He says that the school in itself is not that bad, "but it takes up so much time"—time he would prefer to spend with "friends and stuff." He doesn't like the idea that it begins so early in the morning, and what he "absolutely hates" is the homework. School, he notes, has already taken up a third of his day, and he has a lot of other things to do, including getting a good night's sleep. Some nights he has four hours of homework and when he doesn't have time to finish it all, his grades suffer.[15]

He also plays in the school orchestra and often has rehearsals after school. Then, when he gets home, he needs to call his girlfriend, Cindy, who lives out of town and expects him to call her every night. They usually talk for an hour. So he doesn't get started on his homework until ten or eleven at night. If he doesn't call Cindy, she thinks that he doesn't like her: "I enjoy talking with her but it's just that some nights—like if I've only had three hours of sleep the night before—when I get home I'm just dead tired. All I want to do is go to sleep."[16]

Michael observes that his life is like this all year round. In fall, he has soccer every day after school. In winter, it's the music gala and winter track and basketball. In spring, it's spring track and spring soccer: "There's always an activity after school that I have to go to." In addition, he tries to keep a social life because he likes doing things with friends and going to parties, "but it is hard to keep up."[17]

In some ways, he feels like he doesn't have a personality: "I feel like who I am is just school and soccer and music—just whatever I do. I don't have any time to just be myself." He adds, "I just want to be who I really am, instead of just a collection of all the things I do." He assures Pollack that he doesn't get suicidal, but he does feel depressed at times, and feels like shutting himself off from the world. The way he gets himself out of these depressed moods is to think to himself that he will be able to take

14. Pollack, *Real Boys' Voices*, 155–59. This is the sequel to Pollack's *Real Boys*.
15. Ibid., 155.
16. Ibid.
17. Ibid., 155–56.

it easy in the summer. This helps, but when he gets into one of these moods, they scare him: "They can't be good for me and sometimes I really feel like I could kill someone."[18] He just wishes that he had more time so that he could relax and get more than five hours sleep every night.

Another thing that gets Michael upset is the pressure that his parents put on him. He has an older sister and brother in college and three younger brothers. His sister, Sarah, was a very good student and a big athlete and sports star in high school. His parents, he feels, expect him to do even better, and this is a hard thing to do: "There's this legacy that I have to live up to." He says he was never really close with Sarah but pretty close to his brother Scott—they used to play soccer together—but now that Scott is away at college, he is not much of a part of his life. His next younger brother, Timmy, is the one he is closest too. As for his two youngest brothers, he loves them, but they are just little kids and they really annoy him sometimes, and then he gets angry with them and his temper flares up.[19]

Michael does not say why his parents expect him to do better than Sarah did; nor does he comment on whether Scott was under the same pressure. But, in any case, he feels the pressure of the legacy that Sarah created, which includes being both a very good student and a star athlete. He adds that his parents, besides expecting him to do well in school, also expect him to clean his room and do the dishes when he is home. They say, "Do this" and "do that." He doubts, however, that they understand his frustration with the pressure they place on him, because he doesn't really talk to them much. On the other hand, his parents can tell when he's in a bad mood because he's not very nice to them, and they seem to think that the best thing to do is to leave him alone, that "it's just a teenage thing, a typical boy thing."[20]

He briefly describes his relationships with each parent. Concerning his dad, he doesn't see him much because he's a busy lawyer who is gone a lot because several of the other partners at his firm retired, and he's had to take on all their cases. Since his dad is gone a lot, and he himself is only home to eat, sleep, and do homework, the two of them are sometimes "like two ships passing in the night."[21]

18. Ibid., 156.
19. Ibid., 156–57.
20. Ibid., 157.
21. Ibid.

As for his relationship to his mother, he notes that she is a school guidance counselor, so she knows how to talk to "people like me" better than his dad does; but she tries not to be too pushy and tries to have conversations that she thinks a mother and son ought to have. On the other hand, she likes to "pick away" and find out what he's "up to." She asks questions about his girlfriend and what the two of them have been doing. She also asks about his friends, who his best friend is, and things like that. He says that it doesn't really bother him to tell his mom about what he's been doing, but it sort of annoys him that she's always trying to get into his social life: He feels that he is "sort of on the cusp," that a part of him thinks it's a good thing for her to know who he likes and what he's up to, but another part feels that maybe he'd like to keep his personal life to himself. So when his parents really try to talk to him, he sometimes brushes them off because "I'm just not always in the mood to talk to anyone."[22]

He notes that he has two close friends whom he can, if necessary, talk with about these things, but he usually just keeps things to himself. He feels that the more he talks about what is bothering him, the worse it gets. On the other hand, he sometimes writes things down and is able to describe how he feels and explain the kind of pain and frustration that he has. So he thinks that in the right context he would be capable of talking about how he feels.[23]

He has sometimes thought about going to a professional, but he doesn't think that his problems are *that* bad, and that he really wouldn't know what to say anyway. Then, too, if he began to tell people about how he feels, they would see him as someone who is having serious emotional problems, and this would cause him to "see myself as being less than I am now." There is also his parents' reaction to consider if he were to tell them that he needs to talk to someone. They would get overly worried and instead of just saying, "Oh, we didn't know things were so hard for you," and "Sure, we'll help you out," they'd say, "Oh my God! What's the matter?"[24]

He says he has "two close friends"—Toby is his "best friend"—whom he could really trust and talk to who wouldn't tell anyone else, and who would try to help him as best they could. The problem is that

22. Ibid., 157.
23. Ibid., 158.
24. Ibid., 159.

even they wouldn't really be able to help him much, because talking to someone isn't going to give him a couple more hours in a day to get more sleep at night.

He says that he sometimes feels like he should drop something that he does. But the problem with this is that there isn't anything he doesn't like doing. He doesn't want to give up what he's got going, yet what he's got going is part of what makes him feel overcommitted and pressed. So he tries to live with it. Sometimes he wishes he weren't living this kind of life and that he had more time to himself, but he doesn't really feel in charge of making that happen: "There's all this external pressure and internal pressure. And sometimes I keep myself so busy that I don't even think about it. I guess part of being busy may be to avoid feeling so terrible."[25]

Finally, he thinks that "all of this is something I have to go through," adding that he always figured it would be like this in high school and probably in college too, and that he could then begin to take it slower after he gets a job and starts a family. But that is several years away. Meanwhile, he goes to school, and even if he isn't feeling all that great, he acts like he's having fun and smiles. He keeps a happy face, and other people buy it. But on the inside he feels sad, frustrated, and alone. He concludes on this note: "This one guy, Toby, he and I are best friends. He's real busy too. Maybe I should talk to him."[26]

Michael is clearly a *struggler*. He is making his way through high school and anticipating going on to college, but is doing so with great difficulty. It's not that he is not doing anything well, although he does feel that he is an above-average student who doesn't get time for homework and then gets average grades. The problem is essentially that he is trying to do too many things. He himself uses the word "overcommitted." But if he recognizes this as the problem, he feels helpless to do anything to change it because he is under considerable "external and internal pressure." The external pressure comes from various sources. There are the demands placed on him by the teachers who, he feels, assign too much homework. There are also parental expectations, which are due, in part, to the fact that they want him to do even better than his sister did when she was in high school. And there is his girlfriend, Cindy, who expects him to call her every night. The internal pressures derive from the fact

25. Ibid., 157.
26. Ibid., 159.

that he views himself as an above-average student, but his grades do not always reflect this belief. There is also the fact that he likes the various activities in which he participates after school.

In *Real Boys' Voices,* the book in which Michael's account of his life is presented, William S. Pollack includes an epilogue in which he emphasizes adolescent boys' need for a safe, shame-free zone in which they can go to unwind, let loose, and be their real selves. He also stresses boys' need for at least one mentor on whom they can rely for guidance, love, and support. A mentor may be an adult, but it can be anyone—a mom, a dad, a coach, a buddy, or a girlfriend—"*anyone* who will commit to being there consistently for the boy."[27] Pollack describes the role of the mentor: "This must be a person who listens to him without judgment when he is afraid or in pain; cheers him on as he goes about finding his place in the world; gives him a hug when he feels disappointed in a grade or a game, heartbroken over a troubled friendship, worried or sad about a loss in his life, or disconnected from friends or family."[28]

Pollack adds that "within every family unit, a boy should feel there is at least one mentor upon whom he can count," and, at school, "ideally every boy should know that he has at least one such person upon whom he can regularly rely, whether it is another student his age, an older student, a teacher, counselor, administrator, or school aide." He concludes, "It is absolutely crucial that every boy knows exactly who his mentor is, and for that mentor to be available to him dependably."[29]

Michael is in the awkward position of having several potential mentors, no one of whom seems ideally suited for the role. His mother does what she can to mentor him in the way that Pollack describes, but, despite his observation that she tries to relate to him as a mother, there is a sense in which her professional role as a guidance counselor and her role as his mother are impossible to disentangle. There is also the question whether a mother is likely to be perceived as a person who can listen to her son without appearing to be, at least to some degree, judgmental. It may also be difficult for her not to perceive in his revelations of his struggles that he is being, to some degree, judgmental of her.

As for Michael's father, he has struggles of his own due to the retirements at his law firm and does not seem to have time for his

27. Ibid., 384.
28. Ibid., 384.
29. Ibid.

son. This is especially unfortunate because the very fact that both are struggling and that their struggles are similar (both feel overwhelmed by their various commitments and obligations) could be the basis for a stronger, not lesser bond between them. They could, for example, not only share their struggles but discuss the ways in which they are attempting to deal with them. From such sharing, they might develop a strategy that is mutually beneficial.

Michael's girlfriend, Cindy, does not seem to be capable at this point in her life of mentoring him because she is herself feeling rather insecure about their relationship. She seems to need constant reassurance that he likes her and wants their friendship to continue, and this means that she contributes to his struggles. While it is possible that their conversations over the phone are not as one-way as he represents them to be, that they give him an opportunity to talk about his difficulties and problems, the very fact that she has her own struggles makes it difficult for her to be a mentor to him. To be sure, hardly anyone is *not* struggling with one or another issue or problem. But it places a rather large burden on one adolescent if she or he is to assume the role of mentor to another adolescent. Ask Michael, and he will tell you about the difficulties he experiences in his role as mentor to Cindy.

Given the fact that his sister, Sarah, is the standard against which Michael is expected to measure his achievements, there is little likelihood that she could play the mentor role. His older brother, Scott, might be a better prospect, but the fact of their geographical distance makes this unlikely too.

The possibility of talking with a counselor seems to have occurred to Michael, but he believes, and perhaps rightly so, that were he to do this, he would be perceived by others whose respect for him he values as being "less" than he is now. Pollack suggests that the counseling office should be more visible to high school students (and not hidden behind the health office), and if this were the case at Michael's school, he and other classmates might witness other students going into the center and begin to realize that there is no shame in going in to see a counselor. I think, however, that he might have more difficulties in this regard than some of his classmates because his mother is a guidance counselor. He tells Pollack that she tries hard not to talk to him as a guidance counselor would, and this means that he has some preconceived ideas, perhaps based on his mother's accounts of her work with students, about how school counselors engage in conversation with individual students. It is also possible that she has related to him some of the more difficult cases she has encountered in her role as a guidance counselor, and that this adds to his concern that he could be viewed as more emotionally disturbed than he really is.

Then there is Toby, his best friend, and it's interesting to note that the interview concludes with Michael saying, "He's real busy, too. Maybe I should talk to him." Clearly, Toby would understand and not be judgmental because, after all, he's just as busy as Michael is. Yet, the very fact that Michael has not shared his struggles with Toby in the natural course of their interactions together may indicate a reluctance to burden Toby with his struggles, even as Toby may be reluctant to burden Michael with his struggles.

These reflections are based solely on what Michael has to say in the interview. Pollack, however, was listening carefully to what Michael was saying, and after listening he spoke to Michael about what he had heard. He had become aware as he listened that Michael was exhibiting the classic "boy signs" of depression, "which no adult in his highly educated family or in his sophisticated school had noticed."[30] Pollack explains what these signs were: "He was angry, abusing alcohol, irritable, withdrawn, tempestuous, and engaging in reckless acts of bravado," and "he felt tired a lot of the time and was losing interest in his schoolwork." When Pollack used the word "depression," Michael denied any "depressive" feelings because this was not how he experienced his pain, but as the two of them spoke further, "all the signs emerged."[31] Carefully, in a manner sensitive to his fear and shame, Pollack inquired as to whether he had thought about dying, about taking his own life. Michael thought quietly for a moment and, without confirming Pollack's worries directly, he replied by wondering how Pollack seemed to know about this preoccupation.

Pollack proceeded to explain "the different ways that boys and girls show their sadness and how he [Michael] had many of the signs of depression—even though neither he nor the adults he trusted had recognized or spoken to him about them." He continues: "For the first time during our encounter, some sense of relief—or its potential—entered the room, and Michael asked for my advice. Since suicide was a danger, but

30. Ibid., 150.
31. Ibid.

not an immediate one, I explained that while I could talk to his parents, it would probably be best, if at all possible, if *he* were the one who could broach the issue with his mom and dad."[32] At first Michael was hesitant, explaining that his parents would probably overreact and worry too much, but he agreed to stay in contact with Pollack and gave his permission to speak to others if his own efforts to reach out for help failed.

A few days after they met together one of Pollack's research associates received a call from another boy who had been interviewed from the same community, and he told the research associate that Michael had come to him and to some other boys in town and had told them about his sadness. These boys had given him the support and encouragement he needed to tell his parents how he was really feeling. They, in turn, did not become angry or overreact but were "thrilled" that he had confided in them. Together, as a family, they had begun to see a psychologist who "was helping them work through the feelings of pain that had been bottled up for so long inside of Michael."[33]

As I first read Michael's interview with Pollack, I was impressed by the fact that he could communicate his struggles in an articulate and perceptive manner. I was also struck by the fact that he feels he is capable of describing how he feels in written form and that, given the right context, he can actually talk about how he feels. The interview is itself evidence that this is so. We have also seen how he reached out to his friends after the interview and the conversation with Pollack following

---

32. Ibid.

33. Ibid., 150–51. Michael P. Nichols relates a similar case of a depressed high school boy in *The Self in the System*. Raymond Templeton had confided in the school guidance counselor that he wanted to die. The counselor, who had been working with him for three years, considered this a serious threat and felt that more intensive help than he could provide was called for. So Mrs. Templeton called Nichols's clinic and made an appointment for Raymond. Both parents accompanied him to the first session. Nichols explains that his strategy with Raymond was the customary one of improving the father-son relationship as a wedge to separate the enmeshed mother-son dyad, and then subsequently bring the husband and wife closer together. He relates how despite everyone's best efforts to make this work, the father-son relationship remained rather distant. But Raymond's suicidal thoughts subsided and the therapy with the family was terminated. Several months later Mr. Templeton came to see Nichols for himself. Nichols relates how only through hearing Mr. Templeton's own story did he come to understand why, despite his best intentions, he was unable to connect with his son (3–11). What Pollack in *Real Boys' Voices* calls "the dad connection" (236–48) was hampered in this case by the dad's inadequately developed "self connection."

it, and how this had led to his talking with his parents and to their seeking counseling together.

But given the fact that he is able to describe his feelings in written form, I also wonder if it would help for him to take a course in creative writing as one of his electives. This course may enable him to continue his engagement in writing about his pain and frustration in a form that would not make him uncomfortable. He could, for example, write a short story about a boy who has struggles similar to his own, and perhaps in the very writing of the story he would develop ideas for how he might find an effective way to deal with these struggles.

Pollack, in fact, suggests in his epilogue on mentoring and creating safe spaces that one thing mentors can do is to encourage creative expression. He notes, "As several of the voices that appear in this book reflect, many boys develop emotional awareness and find ways of conveying their vulnerable feelings through writing, art, and music."[34] It is also possible that the class itself would be what Michael calls "the right context" for expressing his feelings. Pollack encourages the creation of many highly accessible safe and shame-free zones where a boy can go "to unwind, let loose, and be his real self."[35] It is quite possible that such a "zone" already exists in the form of a class that encourages the expression of one's feelings through writing.

A possible secondary benefit of a course like this would be that it would encourage the kind of writing that Michael is already doing without thinking of it as "homework." Moreover, by taking this course instead of some other course in order to acquire enough credits to graduate, he may accordingly be reducing the amount of homework that he finds onerous and burdensome. And, conceivably, his enrollment in this course may pique Cindy's interest, and she may find that writing about her own feelings instead of talking about them on the phone every night is inherently self-empowering, such that she does not need to feel quite as vulnerable and in need of Michael's continual reassurances that he is and will be faithful to her.

I realize that I am drawing on my own experience of finding a safe "zone" and a real mentor (the teacher) through a creative writing course when I was in high school. There are obvious dangers in assuming that what worked for oneself as a seventeen-year-old boy would work for

34. Ibid., 389.
35. Ibid., 384.

another seventeen-year-old boy. But I also feel that I know Michael in a way that I do not know many of the other boys in William Pollack's book, for I also recall trying to juggle many interests and responsibilities at that time in my life. I was on the junior varsity baseball team, singing in the school choir, and working as a janitor in the hospital after school. I felt I needed the money so that I could buy and maintain a car because no high school girl would agree to a date with a boy who didn't own his own car. I was also involved in a church youth group, but this was not a context in which one could talk openly about one's struggles. Michael notes that he has two friends with whom he can talk "who wouldn't tell anyone else," which is also to say that there are things he would not confide in the context of a group, even if, as was the case with the church youth group, many of its members were very good friends of mine.

Pollack indicates that the ideal situation is one in which one has a mentor at home and a mentor at school. But like Michael, I felt that an older sibling (in this case, my brother) was the family standard for how I might put my own life together; that my mother, while concerned to have the conversations that she believed a mother and son should have, would not be able to keep my self-disclosures in confidence and would invoke my older brother as a model for me to follow; and that my father, being a traveling accountant who was often out of town from Monday through Friday, would not want to be bothered with my trivial concerns when he was trying, as best he could, to get back into the rhythm of family life over the weekend.

At school, I really had no mentor until I took the creative writing course in my junior and senior years and discovered a mentor in the teacher who taught the course. She introduced us to twentieth-century writers and poets, authors we had never heard of, much less read anything by; and she encouraged us to experiment with many different literary forms—short stories, poems, or essays, for example—and not to be too quick to settle into any single one. As for providing a "shame-free" zone, she invited us to read our work in class, but if any one of us, for whatever reason, was reluctant to do so, she respected this reluctance. She submitted creative writing by several of the students to a scholastic magazine that gave awards for art (paintings, drawings, and sculpture) and writing (poetry, stories, and essays) each year, and my short story was published in the awards issue.[36] When she phoned me at home to tell

36. Capps, "Charlie." In light of the journey theme of this book, it is interesting that

me that the story had been published, I asked her if about several other students in the class whose writing I admired, "Were theirs published too?" She replied, "You need to understand that this was a national competition. The fact that one of my students was selected was a wonderful honor." She added, "I'll see you tomorrow in class."

William Pollack is absolutely right: a reliable mentor and an accessible safe, shame-free zone can make a world of difference in the life of a struggling high school boy. As Stewart, an eighteen-year-old boy from a small town in the South puts it:

> I have always looked up to my music teacher through high school and he is someone who has always been there to talk to. His name is Mr. Forest. He has not only taught music, but he has taught us lessons in life—about how to act and how to be. He has had a really positive influence on everybody who has studied with him. He has always made the right choices. He would never do anything that would hurt anyone else. He looks out for the good of others. He encourages people to be themselves, at least more so than most people. He gives people the opportunity through music to express themselves. I also get close to God through music . . . When I want to get away from it all, get away from all the noise and confusion, I go home and, if no one is there, I go to the piano, or to the organ, and just play whatever is there. Music, for me, is a sanctuary.[37]

Mr. Forest is a music teacher, but he is much more than this. He is a mentor who teaches lessons in life as boys like Stewart and Michael embark on their own personal religious journeys.

Dick: Church Vocation

Dick is a seventeen-year-old boy who is the president of his church youth fellowship.[38] He is a junior in high school, is an outstanding athlete, and quite popular. His parents attend church irregularly and have few other

---

this is a story about a mentally challenged teenage boy named Olav who leaves the mission in western Nebraska where he is being cared for and an older male resident named Charlie who sets out toward the hills in search for him in the belief that the boy knows where he is headed. As the older man, overcome by the heat and physical exertion, falls to the ground, exhausted, he calls out to the boy, "Olav, my boy, I've found you."

37. Pollack, *Real Boys' Voices*, 381.
38. Cryer and Vayhinger, *Casebook in Pastoral Counseling*, 251–57.

affiliations with the church beyond occasional attendance at worship. Dick and his father are apparently very close. His dad is an outdoorsman, and the two of them are always taking hunting and fishing trips together. Both of his parents are college graduates. His mother majored in English and his father in electrical engineering. He is an only child and appears to be especially close to his mother, but now with the help of his dad's outdoor interests, he is becoming more independent of her.

At a youth fellowship meeting the whole evening was devoted to a discussion of vocational choices. Following the discussion Pastor Daniel (called Dan by most of his congregants), a relatively young man in his midthirties in a solo pastorate, passed out index cards and asked the group to write down their vocational interests. When they were handed in, he discovered one that read, "Undecided. Maybe you could help me." It was signed Dick Fielding. After the meeting Dan said to Dick that he would be glad to talk with him about his vocational indecision, and they set a date for the following Saturday morning at ten o'clock.

Dick didn't show up until about 10:20. He apologized for arriving late. He said he had told his mother that he had an appointment with the pastor at ten o'clock, but she insisted that he finish putting up the storm windows. He had been at this task for a week, but now he was finished. He added, "That's one job off my hands." Dan said he was sorry Dick was late because this meant they would have less time to talk together. He asked, "Well, how are things going for you?" Dick replied, "Great. I took first place in shot-put at the tri-district meet last Wednesday. This means I'll get a letter for sure now. I needed sixteen more points to get it and the first place gave me twenty-five more points."[39] Dan expressed his delight in hearing this news and said, "That will give you two letters, won't it?"

Dick replied, "That's right. I got my first one in football last year. Next year I'm going to try and get one in baseball too. If I'm able to get a third letter, it will mean that I can get a blanket at graduation. I'd sure like that. Those blankets are really nice. Have you ever seen one? They're bright red with a big white 'A' in the middle. Wow, are they ever nice."[40]

Dan said that Mr. Wilson, a member of the church, had shown him his once, and agreed that they are really nice. He added, "I'll be plugging

---

39. Ibid., 252.
40. Ibid.

for you Dick; I sure hope you'll be able to get one." He added, "It will make a nice remembrance of your high school days."[41]

Then he changed the subject to the youth fellowship meeting, "Say, wasn't that some discussion we had last Sunday night? I guess the topic of vocations is an important one for everyone."

Dick replied, "I guess it is. Boy, we sure got a big laugh when Joe said he wanted to be a ballet dancer. But I suppose he'd make a good one, he's that type. I'm sure glad you asked me to come today to talk about my vocational choice. I've really been having a rough time deciding what to do."[42] He went on to say that one day he will decide on something then the next week he thinks he'd rather do something else. He added that he has covered three or four different fields "trying to decide what I'd like to do with the rest of my life," but he's getting to the point where he doesn't care anymore: "I'm just going to let nature take its course."

Dan indicated that he can appreciate how Dick feels and asks whether this means he's no longer going to worry about it. Dick replies: "Well, yes and no. I haven't given up all hope, but sometimes my discouragement makes me want to forget the whole thing. In fact, sometimes I even consider forgetting any hopes or ideas of a profession and decide I should get a job as an unskilled laborer of some kind. But I know my parents wouldn't appreciate that. They want me to go to college, and I do want to go, but again I can't decide or make up my mind what to take."[43]

Dan picked up on the conflict Dick feels between wanting to go to college and the discouragement he feels because he really doesn't know what courses to take when he gets there. Dick agreed and added:

> But my parents don't help me much either. If I suggest a certain course to take, they usually don't like it. I once thought I'd like to be a history teacher, but they said I'd be foolish to teach. They said it is not as easy as it looks. But I never said that it looked easy! Then, too, when I was taking physics, I often considered becoming a physicist, but they talked me out of that too. They said that there weren't enough openings in physics and that in order to get into the field one had to be top-notch material. They told me that I wasn't good enough in math to become a top-notch physicist.[44]

41. Ibid.
42. Ibid.
43. Ibid.
44. Ibid., 253.

Dan responded, "So it appears that your parents are squelching any of your ideas about a profession of your own choice." Dick replied, "Yes, all they want me to be is an electrical engineer. My dad could get me in with his company once I have my degree. But I don't want to be an electrical engineer; and, above all, I don't want to be in the same company with Dad. I'd rather do *anything* but electrical engineering, and I'd be glad to work anywhere *except* in the same company as my dad!"[45]

Dan noted that his parents seem to be pushing him into something he doesn't want, and Dick agreed, adding:

> And they dislike any other ideas that I suggest. Mother practically throws a fit at some of my suggestions. For instance, ever since I attended camp between my freshman and sophomore years I have wanted to be a minister. I was convinced at camp that I should be a minister. I had an inner urging to be one. And this urge always seems to come back even when any of the ideas I have fail me. I think I'd rather be a minister than anything else, right now. The first time I told my parents about this my mother let out a howl and cried for an hour or so. When she calmed down she told me I was foolish to think of such things. She claims it is a hard life, that I'd have a lousy salary, that I'd be moving all the time, and a hundred-and-one other arguments against the ministry. She even went so far as to say that I didn't have enough "brains" to be a minister. Dad never said a word that night, but I could tell by his silence that he didn't approve. I told both of them that I had considered the disadvantages of the ministry, but that I was convinced that I'd rather be a minister than anything else. We argued for a while, but finally mother went to her room. That made me feel bad; I hate to see her cry because of me.[46]

Dan commented that despite the fact that the argument made Dick's mother cry and that he feels bad about this, he feels that he would "be happy in the ministry even in face of the disadvantages that your mother pointed out to you."

Dick agreed. "I feel it would be the only place I'd ever be happy with myself. Then, too, it would be the only place I could be on my own for a change. I don't want to wear my dad's shoes; they're too big for me to fill. He's made a name for himself in the company. I'd rather go out

---

45. Ibid., 253.
46. Ibid.

on my own and make a success that way—by myself!"[47] Dan noted the importance for Dick of being his own person, and Dick said yes, but the problem is how to convince his parents:

> I certainly don't want to hurt them, but I don't want to be an electrical engineer. The thing that bothers me is that both my parents have told me they don't think I have what it takes to be a good minister or a good teacher. They say I don't have enough "brains." Yet they seem to think that I could make the grade as an electrical engineer. I can't figure this out. I thought a person would need as much "brains" in the one as in the other. For instance, when I told them I'd like to be a physicist, they said I wasn't good enough in math to be any good as one. But certainly I'd need to be good at math to be a good electrical engineer. That's what I can't figure out. I just wonder if they aren't trying to talk me into electrical engineering. I don't like being suspicious of them, but sometimes I just can't help it.[48]

He went on to relate what happened last month on his birthday: "I asked that they give me a copy of the Revised Standard Version of the New Testament. But they didn't; they gave me a shirt and some ties instead. They had all kinds of excuses for not giving the New Testament to me. But I know darn well they didn't want me to have it. I shouldn't say things like that, but sometimes I just can't help it. I hate to be suspicious of them—it makes me feel bad about feeling this way."[49]

Then, noting that he sometimes thinks it would "be better for me to run away from home and live my life as I would like to live it, and without anyone telling me what to do all the time," he asked Dan whether everyone who enters the ministry has as many problems as he has had, and added, "If they do it sure is surprising how many are in the ministry." Then he asked point blank what he should do: "Should I go along with my parents and forget the ministry, which would be very hard for me to do, or should I just revolt from them and do as I please? I realize that the Bible says we should honor our fathers and our mothers, but I also know that Jesus suggested that we might have to stand against our own parents. What do you think I should do? What would you do if you were in my place?"[50]

47. Ibid, 253–54.
48. Ibid., 254.
49. Ibid.
50. Ibid., 254–55.

Trying hard not to give Dick direct advice, Dan said that he couldn't really tell him what he would do because what he himself would do may not be the thing for Dick to do: "Each situation involves a different personality, so we can't draw any general plans of action. We each have to meet our problems as our own individual problems, and ours alone."[51] Dick said that he supposed this is the case, but was wondering if others have had the same problem that he is having, or "am I the only fish in the brook with this kind of trouble." Dan said that it's hard to say, but that "our time is up for today," so "maybe you'd like to think some more about your problem of making a decision as to what to do and then we could talk together some more."[52]

Dick replied that he felt better already for having talked with Dan, and asked if he could come again next Saturday morning: "I'll try to be on time, so then maybe we could come to some definite conclusions."[53] Dan agreed and added that he'd see Dick at the youth fellowship tomorrow evening.

In his comments on the conversation, Dan notes that although Dick is "visibly close to his dad, he refuses very strongly to be associated with him in any way in business. He places his individuality on a higher plane of value." He also suggests that Dick "is able to make some profound observations; for example, he recognizes the incongruity of his parents' thinking." On the other hand, he suggests that there is a certain incongruity in the fact that "although he continually stresses the fact that he wants freedom from authority so that he might live his life as he so chooses, he nevertheless seeks an answer from me as to what he should do in regard to his problems."[54]

In their comments on the conversation, David D. Eitzen and Carroll Wise, both of whom were seminary professors in pastoral psychology at the time, tend to agree with Dan's observation that Dick seems to want to force the pastor into being an authority figure. Eitzen suggests that were the pastor to have agreed to this, he would have fallen prey to "the boy's repeated attempts to use him as a substitute mother." Similarly, Wise suggests we take a careful look at the "dynamics" of this boy:

---

51. Ibid., 255.
52. Ibid.
53. Ibid.
54. Ibid.

> He is rebelling against pressure and authority; yet he asks the pastor to be his authority and give him an answer. This is typical of adolescents of all ages. Had the pastor given the answers, he would have kept the boy in an immature relationship and would have become involved in the rebellion. With the process of understanding and acceptance, he helps the boy to work into his feelings and to find his authority in life itself rather than in an older person. The vocational problem is primarily a symptom of a deeper problem. This deeper problem (the boy's relationship with his parents and the growth of his own personality) will take more time to work through.[55]

He adds that the solution will come through a continuation of the relationship started in this conversation and that Dick "can grow emotionally and spiritually only through a secure relationship with the pastor" that allows him "the freedom to work out his problems and find his own answers." In this way, "the pastor can mediate the love of God to this boy."[56]

Eitzen also picks up on the pastor's observation that Dick has been especially close to his mother, and suggests that his "chief difficulty is his history of finding his sense of security in pleasing his mother." He also notes that the initial discussion of Dick's athletic interests and his comment about the boy who wanted to become a ballet dancer implies that he "wants desperately to achieve male-hood." He suggests that Dan "might have capitalized upon the boy's success in athletics by suggesting that perhaps he would want to choose athletics as a vocation," but notes that the approach he took enabled him "to indicate one of his fears; namely, that he too might be 'that type'—meaning effeminate." In any event, it is clear that "he identifies with his hunter father," but the problem is that "the father turns out to be as possessing as his mother" who "put him over the barrel by weeping when he asserted his individuality." Eitzen exclaims, "What could be more emasculating!"[57]

As in the case of Michael, the boy's need for a mentor is especially prominent in Dick's case as well. Although, as both Eitzen and Wise point out, the pastor is to be commended for refusing to be set up to be another authority figure in Dick's life, it seems rather apparent that Dick wanted to know if his struggles relating to his desire to become a min-

55. Ibid., 257.
56. Ibid.
57. Ibid., 256.

ister were atypical, or whether this was a rather common experience. I doubt that Dan would have been allowing himself to get "set up" as an authority figure if he had responded to this question in a straightforward manner. A full self-disclosure would not have been necessary, but an acknowledgment that he had struggles, perhaps similar in nature, would have enabled Dick to feel that, although, as Gordon Allport emphasizes, "the religious quest of the individual is solitary,"[58] this does not mean that this individual is the first to have struck out on this quest, nor need it mean that he is without companions along the way.

As William Pollack puts it, a boy needs a mentor on whom "he can rely for guidance, love, and support."[59] For Dan to have answered Dick's question as to whether others have had to struggle so hard against parental pressure in a straightforward way (i.e., in the affirmative) would be congruent with the mentor's role of providing guidance and support. Also, in light of Dick's disappointment that his parents did not give him a Revised Standard Version of the New Testament (which was then a new translation) it would be appropriate for Dan to draw Dick's attention to Mark 1:16–20:

> And passing along by the Sea of Galilee, he saw Simon and Andrew the brother of Simon casting a net in the sea; for they were fishermen. And Jesus said to them, 'Follow me and I will make you become fishers of men.' And immediately they left their nets and followed him. And going on a little farther, he saw James the son of Zebedee and John his brother, who were in their boat mending the nets. And immediately he called them; and they left their father Zebedee in the boat with the hired servants, and followed him. (RSV)

Was their decision to follow Jesus a failure to *honor* their father by not remaining fishermen? To *honor* means to respect a person who is deserving of respect. But *honor* is not synonymous with *deference*, which means to yield to the claims or wishes of a person whom one respects.[60]

Dan might point out that he does not perceive in Dick any evidence of a lack of respect for his father and mother. For one thing, he has related that a major reason why he does not want to become an electrical engineer is that he doesn't want "to wear my dad's shoes; they're too

---

58. Allport, *The Individual and His Religion*, 141–42.
59. Pollack, *Real Boys' Voices*, 384.
60. Agnes, ed., *Webster's New World*, 685.

big for me to fill."⁶¹ Does this sound like a son who does not respect his father? Also, what about the fact that he was twenty minutes late for their conference because his mother insisted that he finish putting up the storm windows even though she knew that Dan would be expecting Dick to come at ten o'clock? Does this sound like a son who is disrespectful toward his mother? If I were Dan, I might point out that in Mark's version of the story, James and John did not leave their father to carry on the family fishing business all by himself, for there were, after all, hired servants to help him (Matt 4:22 leaves this important detail out). Similarly, it is not as if Dick would be creating a hardship for his dad if he didn't come back to work in the same company.

It might also be appropriate to add that Jesus is not showing disrespect for the occupation of the fisherman by calling these four men to join him. On the contrary, he uses this very occupation as a metaphor for what he is calling them to become—fishers of men. Perhaps, then, Dick could explore ways in which his father's occupation as an electrical engineer might provide insights into how he might understand the profession he has wanted to pursue ever since he attended camp between his freshman and sophomore years. Perhaps while he and his dad are on hunting or fishing trips together, he could ask his dad about what he has learned about life and himself through his profession as an electrical engineer.

In time, Dan might also provide Dick guidance for how to deal with the fact that his mother is deeply threatened by the prospect that her son will move away and that she will be left alone. Her role in causing Dick to be late for his appointment, her desire that he become an electrical engineer so that he could work in his father's company and thereby live close by, her observation that ministers move around a lot—all these point to the fact that she is struggling with the fact that he is likely to leave home permanently, regardless what profession he chooses. Dick's own observation that he sometimes feels that "it would be better for me to run away from home" reflects his unconscious awareness that his mother cannot bear to see him go.

I believe that Dan could help Dick develop one or another strategy for addressing this aspect of Dick's struggle to find his own way without dishonoring his parents. If Dick aspires to become a minister, perhaps

61. Cryer and Vayhinger, *Casebook in Pastoral Counseling*, 253.

Dan can help him to see how a minister might be supportive to his mother in adjusting to the inevitable loss of her son's daily presence.

He might, perhaps, mention that in the Gospel of Mark, James and John, the sons of Zebedee, come to Jesus and ask to sit at his right and left when he ascends to his own place of glory (Mark 10:35–45) but in the Gospel of Matthew it is their mother who makes this request in their behalf (Matt 20:20). They might discuss her role in the story and what her motivations might be. Perhaps she is ambitious for her sons. But whatever her motivations might be, Jesus tells them that in his "company" the usual lines of authority are reversed:

> You know that those who are supposed to rule over the Gentiles lord it over them and their great men exercise authority over them. But it shall not be so among you; but whoever would be great among you must be your servant, and whoever would be first among you must slave of all. For the Son of man came not to be served but to serve, and to give his life as a ransom for many. (Mark 10:42–45; also Matt 20:25–28 RSV).

In drawing Dick's attention to this story, Dan would also be addressing Dick's suggestion that the ministry would not only be the place where he'd "be happy with myself," but would also be the only place "I could be on my own for a change," and "make a success that way—by myself!"[62]

Dick has had opportunity to gain some sense of what a minister is and does by observing Dan, and this would probably dispel many of the possible illusions he might have about the profession he feels he wants to pursue. But the story told in Mark 10:35–45 and Matt 20:20–28 makes clear that the "place" Dick wants to be in is one in which he may feel that he is "on his own," but only because his acceptance of the invitation of Jesus to follow him has freed him from the obligation to do what his parents want him to do with his life. Moreover, he will be choosing a profession in which "success" is not a matter of making a "name" for oneself. In fact, Dan might suggest that Dick ask his father to give him a tour of his company and while doing so, to observe the custodial staff cleaning the sinks and toilets in the restrooms, picking up the empty bottles and cans that others have carelessly left on the tables and floors,

62. Ibid., 253–54.

and emptying the trash. As this would be a living parable, Dan would not need to make the point explicit.[63]

Dan may also provide Dick guidance for how to deal with the fact that, although his father may not have the same emotional investment in keeping Dick close by, it seems by his silence that he doesn't approve of his son's desire to become a minister. He also remains silent when his wife suggests that a person needs more "brains" to be a minister than to be an electrical engineer, and adds that she doubts her son has the necessary "brains." She seems here to put her husband down. Here too Dan might help Dick to see how a minister might assist his dad to express his thoughts and feelings more openly. Also, it is quite conceivable that he too fears the day when Dick leaves home and there is no one to provide an emotional buffer between himself and his wife (who, as Dick's description of the argument over his announcement that he wanted to become a minister indicates, is prone to emotional manipulation).

It is not, of course, Dick's role to be his parents' minister. Nor is Dan's role to explain to him how he would go about ministering to them if they sought his counsel. But he could indicate to him how he perceives the dilemma that Dick is in, and help him to see that a minister's role may well be to understand what Dick refers to as the "confusing" signals that he is receiving from his parents.

Finally, if Dick is able to rely on Dan as his mentor, he may not feel the need to talk with his parents about his professional future. As his account of these conversations indicates, they tend to result in arguments that cause everyone to feel frustrated and upset. Since Dick is a boy who is just striking out on his religious journey, this may not be the time to engage in discussion with his parents about where his ultimate destination lies. In fact, at this point in his life, Dick does not know where his ultimate destination may be. This does not mean, however, that Dan needs to parry Dick's desire to achieve some clarity about what lies out

---

63. An illustration of the use of a living parable in counseling in Milton H. Erickson's "Cacti" case in Rosen, *My Voice Will Go with You*. In this case, Erickson advised a man who was an alcoholic to go to the Botanical Gardens across town and "look at all the cacti there and marvel at cacti that can survive for three years without water, without rain. And do a lot of thinking." Years later the man's daughter came to Erickson's office. She said that she wanted to meet the counselor who "would send an alcoholic out to the Botanical Gardens to look around, to learn how to get around without alcohol, and have it work" (80–81). Erickson may also have been playing on the rhyme between "a lot of thinking" and "a lot of drinking."

ahead of him. In the previous chapter I quoted these lines from John Henry Newman's poem "The Pillar of the Cloud":

> Keep Thou my feet; I do not ask to see
> The distant scene—one step enough for me.[64]

But Newman was at sea when he wrote these words, and in a similar way Dick too seems to be at sea. The youth group laughed when Joe said he wanted to be a ballet dancer, but at least Joe knows what he wants to be. In contrast, Dick wrote on his index card, "Undecided. Maybe you could help me." When a ship is at sea and darkness is everywhere, the fact that there is a light from the lighthouse on the shore provides reassurance that, at least, the ship is not in danger of colliding against the rocks on the nearby shore.

In expressing his appreciation for the chance to talk with Dan and his request for another opportunity the following week, Dick said that he would "try to be on time, so then maybe we could come to some definite conclusions." Dan responded rather vaguely, "Well, we'll see what we can do." Thus, whereas Dick attributes the indeterminate outcome of this conversation to the fact that it was abbreviated due to his having come late, Dan's response indicates that he does not anticipate that they will, in fact, reach any "definite conclusions." Although both Eitzen and Wise believe that Dick has some issues that will take time to work out Wise does say that "at certain points the pastor might have been clearer in his responses."[65] I agree. Dick is desperately seeking clarity, and Dan can help him find clarity in the midst of confusion. If Wise believes that the pastor can mediate the love of God to him, this very mediation may take the form of helping him to see more clearly where he is going.

This might involve finding out more about what education for the ministry involves. It might even involve finding out about the very issues that his mother has raised as objections to his becoming a minister, such as their salaries in comparison to those of electrical engineers, how often ministers typically move from one church to another, and so forth. This research would probably not be useful arguing points with his parents, for it may well confirm that she is right. And even if it were to challenge these arguments, she, as Dick puts it, would come up with "a hundred-and-one other arguments against the ministry." This research, however,

---

64. Newman, *Verses on Various Occasions*, 156.
65. Cryer and Vayhinger, *Casebook in Pastoral Counseling*, 257.

may help him gain a better measure of his own inner desire to become a minister and not resign himself completely to what he calls "letting nature take its course."[66]

William Pollack points out that a reliable mentor cheers a boy on "as he goes about finding his place in the world."[67] Because, for Dick, this quest is clearly a religious quest, Gordon Allport's concluding words in *The Individual and His Religion* provide an apt conclusion to our consideration here of the struggles of three adolescent boys—Augustine, Michael, and Dick: "A man's religion is the audacious bid he makes to bind himself to creation and to the Creator," his "ultimate attempt to enlarge and complete his own personality by finding the supreme context in which he rightly belongs."[68]

66. Ibid., 252–53.
67. Pollack, *Real Boys' Voices*, 384.
68. Allport, *The Individual and His Religion*, 142.

3
The Straggler

IN THE INTRODUCTION I noted that a *straggler* is a person who strays from the path or course, wanders from the main group, or falls behind the others. I suggested that this experience is relevant to teenage boys because some boys often, and others occasionally, find it difficult to keep up with the others, whether scholastically, socially, or physically. Unlike the *stumbler*, it is not so much a case of being awkward, confused, or susceptible to falling, but rather a case of moving along at a slower pace due, in part, to slower maturation or to being interested in things that are not of central interest to the majority of teenagers.

I also noted that the *stumbler, struggler,* and *straggler* form a trio because they portray the boy as having difficulty moving forward on the journey and staying up with the others. Like the *stumbler and struggler,* the *straggler* may be feeling rather isolated and alone on the journey. On the other hand, he may be joined by one or more other *stragglers*, and he and they may chose to walk together, united, as it were, in their tendency to fall behind the ones who are setting the pace.

I suggested that, as with the other four vulnerabilities of adolescence, the *straggler* role is not necessarily negative (or wholly so). The *straggler* may find that his distraction from what others consider important is something well worth noticing and finding out more about. The others may fail to notice what he notices because they are too concerned to move along and maintain their pace. As we will see in this chapter, the *straggler* is often the one who peers more deeply and concentrates more fully on important things than the others do. This is more likely to be the case if his straggling has a purpose other than the pleasure of irritating the pacesetters by means of the rather passive-aggressive act of foot-dragging.

Henry David Thoreau: Different Drummer

Scott A. Sandage begins his book *Born Losers* with an account of the funeral of Henry David Thoreau (who had died of tuberculosis on May 6, 1862).[1] Ralph Waldo Emerson (who was fourteen years older than Thoreau) was the eulogist. The townsfolk and visiting notables who crowded into the First Parish Church in Concord, Massachusetts, heard the eulogist admit what many had thought all along: that the dearly departed had wasted his gifts. Emerson lamented: "He seemed born for greatness . . . and I cannot help counting it a fault in him that he had no great ambition." Rather than an engineer or a general, "he was the captain of a huckleberry-party," and when he wasn't picking berries, he had tried his hand at a variety of occupations: teacher, surveyor, pencil maker, housepainter, mason, farmer, gardener, and writer. In effect, Sandage notes, Emerson said that his friend's "quirky ambitions did not amount to a hill of beans."[2]

However, Sandage also points out that Thoreau's *Walden* concludes with his own response to his critics. Thoreau asks, "Why should we be in such desperate haste to succeed, and in such desperate enterprises? If a man does not keep pace with his companions, perhaps it is because he hears a different drummer."[3] He adds: "Let him step to the music which he hears, however measured or far away. It is not important that he should mature as soon as an apple-tree or an oak."[4]

In effect, Thoreau was a self-admitted *straggler*. But he was thirty-seven years old when he wrote *Walden*. Was he a *straggler* in his teenage years? I believe that he was, and that others his own age would have agreed.

Born in 1817, Henry David Thoreau was the third of four children of John and Cynthia Thoreau. His sister Helen was five years and his brother John was three years older. He had a younger sister, Sophia. His father, who was thirty-six years old when Henry was born, had begun

1. Sandage, *Born Losers*.
2. Ibid., 1–2.
3. Thoreau, *Walden*, 20.
4. Ibid., 255.

his occupational life as a merchant. But he failed in business and lost whatever he inherited from his father. So he turned his attention to pencil making, a trade to which he had been introduced a decade or so earlier. He was an excellent pencil maker and this trade provided an adequate living for himself and his family.

Henry Salt, an early biographer,[5] describes Thoreau's preteen years as ones in which he spent a lot of time in the natural world surrounding the village of Concord. He enjoyed bathing, fishing and boating on the Concord River and would join the other village boys and girls when a canal-boat laden with lime, bricks, and iron ore would glide along the river so that they could see the river-men who came and went. There were also the remnants of Native American tribes who would pitch their tents in the rich meadows that had belonged to their ancestors. They taught the village children how to string beads and weave baskets and initiated the older ones into the art of paddling a canoe.[6]

As a child Thoreau was afraid of thunderstorms and would go to his father for protection. But most of the anecdotes from his early youth indicate that he was fearless, self-reliant, and noted for the brevity of his speech. When he was accused of taking a knife belonging to another boy, he said simply, "I did not take it," and refused to defend himself any further. Eventually, the true offender was identified. When he was ten years old, he took some pet chickens to sell to a neighboring innkeeper who, in order to return the basket immediately, wrung their necks before Henry's eyes, and although he watched with outraged feelings, he did not say a word.[7]

Thoreau was sent to Harvard University in the fall of 1833. He had just turned sixteen. He had been prepared for college at the Concord Academy, a school known for its emphasis on the Greek classics. His expenses at Harvard were a serious concern for his parents, whose financial means were limited, but these difficulties were surmounted by his own carefulness and economy and by the help of his aunts and his elder

---

5. Salt, *Life of Henry David Thoreau*. He wrote the original version in 1890. A revised version was published in 1896. A third version was completed in 1908 and was published in 1993 through the efforts of editors George and Willene Hendrick and Fritz Oehlschlager. Walter Harding is quoted on the dust jacket: "Of all the biographers of Thoreau, Henry Salt best captures Thoreau's spirit ... [This book] is astoundingly up to date because Salt wrote it more as a spiritual than as a factual biography."

6. Ibid., 6.

7. Ibid., 7.

sister, Helen, who was a schoolteacher at this time. During his sophomore year, he took a leave of absence and taught at a school in Canton, Massachusetts. His junior year was further broken up by absence and illness. He returned in March 1836 but became ill and withdrew in May, before the end of term. When he returned in the fall of 1836, he took three straight terms and graduated in 1837.[8]

A classmate, the Reverend John Weiss, later described Thoreau in the *Christian Examiner* (1865) as a loner. He noted that he did not share in other students' studies and amusements, or attend their oyster suppers and wine parties. He would mysteriously disappear when the other boys would engage in an occasional "rebellion" against college discipline. Weiss also noted that the touch of Henry's hand was moist and indifferent as if he had just picked up something when he saw the other person's hand coming. There was also something peculiar about his walk: "The prominent blue-eyes seemed to rove down the path, just in advance of his feet, as his grave Indian stride carried him down to University Hall." Also, "his eyes were sometimes searching as if he had dropped, or expected to find, something. In fact, his eyes seldom left the ground, even in his most earnest conversations with you." Weiss also implies that Thoreau was not ready for college: "thought had not yet awakened his countenance; it was serene, but rather dull, rather plodding." Moreover, "he would smile to hear the word 'collegiate career' applied to the reserve and inaptness of his college life."[9]

Henry Salt notes that Thoreau seemed uninterested in the honors that fall to the successful student. Weiss notes that his classmates did not attribute his aloofness and self-seclusion to conceit, still less to shyness, but to "a sort of homely 'complacency,' which, though quite natural and inevitable, had the effect of putting him out of sympathy with his surroundings at Harvard." By "complacency," Salt means that he would not do anything to ingratiate himself with the faculty and his classmates, for they had little if any significance for him. In his view, Thoreau's determined concentration on his own life course, a characteristic of his later career, is evident at this early stage.[10]

Having gotten his Harvard degree at age twenty, what did he do next? He returned to Concord in 1837 and took a teaching position in

8. Richardson, *Henry Thoreau: A Life of the Mind*, 11–12.
9. Salt, *Life of Henry David Thoreau*, 10.
10. Ibid., 11.

a grammar school that had recently been established. This position was short-lived, however, because he objected to the policy laid down by the School Committee that he must use the stick he had been provided for punishing students and not substitute physical punishment by "talking morals."[11] In the spring of 1838 he went to Maine, where his mother had relatives, in search of a teaching position. But even though he had reference letters from Emerson, the local pastor George Ripley, and the president of Harvard, he was unsuccessful in finding a job. He returned home.

Salt notes that the "question of a profession, it may well be supposed, was pressed on the youthful enthusiast by anxious relatives and friends."[12] Since his father had taught him how to make pencils, he began making pencils, and everyone felt that he had at last found his true profession. But he suddenly declared that he wouldn't make another pencil and decided that he would become a professional walker or "saunterer," as he called it. He would spend at least one half of each day in the open air, watching the dawns and sunsets, securing the latest news from the forests and hilltops, and serving, as he put it, as "self-appointed inspector of snow storms and rain storms." Given his familiarity with the surroundings, his services were often requested for land surveying, but he mostly supported himself over the next decade as a manual laborer.[13]

Salt observes that his relatives had higher ambitions for him; but he cites Thoreau's poem titled "Prayer," in which he asks the "Great God" for nothing less than that "I may not disappoint myself," then asks that God would also grant that he "may greatly disappoint my friends." Why? Because whatever they think or hope he might become, they have no conception of who he is in the sight of God.[14]

Salt also notes that Thoreau was extremely loyal to his older brother John, and when he sensed that John shared his feelings for Ellen Sewell, who would come to Concord from her home in Scituate to visit her own brothers, he deferred to his brother. As it turned out, Ellen was not romantically attracted to either of them, and she eventually married a clergyman.[15] When he was twenty-five, John died suddenly and painfully of lock-jaw, caused by an injury to his hand while shaving. Thoreau

11. Ibid., 15.
12. Ibid., 17.
13. Ibid., 18–19.
14. Ibid., 19.
15. Ibid., 21.

is said to have turned pale and faint when narrating the circumstances of his brother's death to a friend more than twelve years later. A friend who knew them both later wrote that after his brother's death, Thoreau "seemed to have no earthly companion in whom he could confide and love; he appeared indifferent to all around him, and sometimes I thought he even hated himself." In a letter written two months after his brother's death, he wrote that he had no right to grieve because "only Nature has a right to grieve perpetually, for she only is innocent."[16]

When Thoreau and Emerson met is unknown, but Emerson moved to Concord in 1834, and knew Thoreau well enough in Thoreau's senior year to write the president of Harvard that year on his behalf for a scholarship. Robert Sattelmeyer notes that when Thoreau returned to Concord after he graduated from Harvard, Emerson gave Thoreau advice and encouragement with his writing projects, lobbied publishers and editors on his behalf, advanced him money, and provided him a place to live and the leisure to write. Over time, despite the fact that Thoreau exceeded Emerson's expectations in some ways, he was also "a puzzle and disappointment to Emerson," and at the same time, Emerson himself "changed in ways that caused him to decline in Thoreau's estimation." Yet, it was Emerson who gave Thoreau permission to build a cabin on the land he had recently purchased on Walden Pond, and it was there that Thoreau took up residence in the summer of 1845 and proceeded to write *Walden*.[17]

Emerson wrote a long essay based on his eulogy at Thoreau's funeral. In it, he notes that Thoreau graduated from Harvard College in 1837, "but without any literary distinction," then "joined his brother in teaching [in] a private school, which he soon renounced." Then he took up his father's trade of making pencils, "believing he could make a better pencil than was then in use," and when he completed his experiments, "he exhibited his work to chemists and artists in Boston, and having obtained their certificates to its excellence and to its equality with the best London manufacture, he returned home contented." His friends "congratulated him that he had now opened his way to fortune," but he replied that he would never make another pencil: "Why should I? I would not do again what I have done once." He resumed his "endless walks and miscellaneous studies, making every day some new acquaintance with

16. Ibid., 27.
17. Sattelmeyer, "Thoreau and Emerson," 25–39.

nature," but he never spoke about zoology or botany, for although he was "very studious of natural facts," he lacked any curiosity about technical and textual science.[18]

Emerson went on to note that at this time "all his companions were choosing their profession, or eager to begin some lucrative employment." It was inevitable that Thoreau's thoughts would be "exercised on the same question, and it required rare decision to refuse all the accustomed paths and keep to his solitary freedom at the cost of disappointing the natural expectations of his family and friends." But in this decision he "never faltered." He refused "to give up his large ambition of knowledge and action for any narrow craft or profession, aiming at a much more comprehensive calling, the art of living well." Never idle or self-indulgent, when he needed money, he would earn it "by some piece of manual labor agreeable to him, as building a boat or a fence, planting, grafting, surveying, or other short work."[19]

Emerson added that Thoreau never married, lived alone, ate vegetables and fruit, never drank alcohol or smoked, and refused invitations to dinner parties because "they make their pride in making their dinner cost much; I make my pride in making my dinner cost little." When he was asked what dish he preferred, he answered, "the nearest." He was not the easiest person to be with because he would rather disagree than agree with whatever anyone else said. A friend once commented, "I love Henry, but I cannot like him; and as for taking his arm, I should as soon think of taking the arm of an elm tree."[20] We can well imagine that had Thoreau heard him say this, he would have responded, "Then do so."

What especially stands out in Emerson's essay is how Thoreau determined his own pace wherever he went, and that he was so carefully observant of whatever he encountered on his walks. Nothing escaped his eyes. And because he saw so much, he was convinced that there was no need to take trips to far-off lands because there was so much to see and learn about in the vicinity of Concord.

Thoreau was a *straggler*. He was a person who strayed from the path or course, who wandered from the main group, and who fell behind the others. He made no effort to keep up, for, in a sense, he had nowhere to go, no destination to reach. But, as Emerson emphasizes, he was never

18. Emerson, "Thoreau," 351–52.
19. Ibid., 352.
20. Ibid., 353.

idle or self-indulgent. He was as fully engaged as anyone in the village of Concord. Because he was a *straggler*, it is not surprising that he enjoyed the company of younger persons. As Emerson notes, "Yet, hermit and stoic as he was, he was really fond of sympathy, and threw himself heartily and childlike into the company of young people whom he loved, and whom he delighted to entertain, as he only could, with the varied and endless anecdotes of his experiences by field and river: and he was always ready to lead a huckleberry-party or a search for chestnuts or grapes."[21] To the children, he was not a *straggler*; he was a leader.

Thus, Thoreau was a sort of professional *straggler*. He made a career of *straggling*. As Sandage notes, Emerson was not entirely laudatory in his eulogy at Thoreau's funeral. He feels that if Thoreau's genius had only been contemplative, he was ideally suited for the life he lived, "but with his energy and practical ability he seemed born for great enterprise and for command." If he had combined ambition with his "rare powers of action," instead of being the captain of a huckleberry-party, he could have been an engineer for all America. Still, although he scoffed at conventional elegance, he had many elegancies of his own: "Thus, he could not bear to hear the sound of his own steps, the grit of gravel; and therefore never willingly walked in the road, but in the grass, on mountains and in woods."[22]

The *straggler* is typically a person who refuses to walk the road that others are travelling. To them, he has fallen behind. To him, they need to learn to stray from the beaten path, to take a chance on getting lost. Having taken that chance, Thoreau could not have gotten lost if he tried. And as Emerson notes: "He could find his path in the woods at night, he said, better by feet than his eyes."[23]

We need, however, to be careful not to overly romanticize Thoreau's *straggler* identity. During his later teens, the period of his life that especially interests us here, he was a college student. He was only a few miles from home, but by any normal standard, his college years were not especially good ones. He left college in his sophomore year to take a teaching position, and when he returned in his junior year, he had to withdraw due to illness. Having fallen behind, he needed to enroll in an extra term in order to graduate on time. Emerson notes that he seldom expressed

21. Ibid., 354.
22. Sandage, *Born Losers*, 367.
23. Emerson, "Thoreau," 357.

appreciation for his college education, holding it in small esteem, even though, in Emerson's own view, his debt to the college was important.[24]

If Thoreau had had a better experience in college, it is very possible that he would have developed the ambitions that Emerson feels were lacking in him and would have made greater use of his energy and practical ability. Of course, we can argue that if Thoreau had kept up with the others during his college days, the nation would have lost one of its most celebrated authors and role models. Still, the *straggler* is likely to be subject to criticism and ostracism by his classmates, and although he may claim that his ostracism is self-chosen, it may well be the case that such claims reflect an attempt to put a positive face on an unpleasant or undesirable situation.

Francis and Kirk: Two Distinct Profiles

As we shift our focus to the contemporary teenage boy, I will focus on two interviews presented by William S. Pollack.[25] These interviews, when compared, enable us to see how the boy who fits the identity or role of the *straggler* contrasts with the boy who is moving forward on the path of life toward a discernible future. Francis is the boy who presents himself as moving forward, and doing so with considerable clarity about the person he wants to be as he moves into adulthood. Kirk is the boy who believes that he has certain deficiencies that cause him to doubt whether he will be able to keep up with the others.

Pollack's interview with Francis, an eighteen-year-old boy living in a suburb in the Northwest, is titled "The American Dream." This title picks up on the fact that Francis begins by noting that his dad has been very successful, and that he "epitomizes the American dream." He adds, "Subconsciously, his success probably does rub off on me a bit. But I don't go to school thinking, 'Oh God, I have to get into a top college so I can fill my dad's shoes.' Actually, I think how it effects me is by making me want to distance myself from him. I wouldn't want to follow his career steps or have to live up to his image. I want a sense of accomplishment that is completely independent of him."[26]

---

24. Ibid., 351.
25. Pollack, *Real Boys' Voices*.
26. Ibid., 56–57.

Francis goes on to say that his dad's role as the family provider was predominant over all other paternal roles. He suggests that the provider role has been genetically bred into us over the millennia: "The male is supposed to make sure that his family is protected and adequately provided for. And my dad was disappointed that he couldn't come to my games, but at the same time he felt that he had to provide. That was his job, and he couldn't fail at it. I don't hold it against him because something in me realizes that that was the role the man had to play for so long. I am just not sure it will be the path I will take."[27]

He anticipates having "more of a human connection" with his own children when that time comes, and he believes that "you can find a way for both your career and your family. By prioritizing things, there is room for both." He concludes: "You just have to evaluate what is really important and what really matters in life. I want to be able to look back on my life and say, 'I'm proud of what I did, I'm proud of how I raised my children. I'm proud of what I meant as a person.' My advice to people is to just make sure that you are proud of what you decide to do, so that you can look back and say with sincerity, 'I made the right decisions.'"[28]

Clearly, Francis has been thinking about the future and the path that he will follow. He has even thought about how he wants to be able to look back on the journey he has taken. He thinks of himself as having both a career and a family, and has already given thought to how he wants to make room for both. In reading the interview, one has a sense that he is a mature boy who has looked down the path that he will follow and, in his mind at least, he has already set out on the journey.

A few of the boys interviewed by Pollack present a very different picture. They are much more caught up in the present and seem not to be thinking a whole lot about the future; or, if they do think about it, they don't look forward to it with any sense of anticipation. They do not use the word *straggler* in reference to themselves, but there is sense in which they feel that they are not keeping up with the others or are striking out on their own path, one that has little if any association with the American dream, however that dream is understood or defined.

Like Francis, Kirk is an eighteen-year-old boy from a suburb in the Northwest. The interview is titled "Alone." The interview with Francis occurs in the chapter of *Real Boys' Voices* titled "The Angst of Becoming

27. Ibid., 57.
28. Ibid., 57–58.

a Man: Coming of Age." The interview with Kirk is in the chapter titled "Addictions: Drugs, Alcohol, and the Media." Here is how it begins: "I'm not very happy. I was recently accepted into college, and now I have just started to slack off. It's been hell for four years, but I'm almost through. At least school is better than it was last year, when I was sure I wasn't going to get into college. I'm pushing myself for two more months, and then it's done."[29]

Kirk then moves into a discussion of his drug use: "My friends and I do a lot of drugs. We get high on everything. We drink a lot and smoke weed. Drugs that I've seen at my school are Ecstasy, cocaine, mushrooms, alcohol, and pot. I've done Ecstasy, but I don't do it now. I smoke pot and drink. I'm addicted to pot and I have my share of problems with it. Sometimes I think it burns me out. I always want to smoke and when I try to quit, I can't. I start to wonder what my life would be like without it."[30]

He adds that he and all of his friends experiment, but they limit it to coke and Ecstasy:

> Ecstasy is the drug of our generation. The grossest thing about it is that the next day I feel retarded. My body feels like a piece of shit. When I'm on Ecstasy, I don't talk and I'm not myself. That's what I noticed the last time I was on it. I have one friend that we call the "Gnome," because when she does drugs, she puts on her hood and hides under the blankets. She just watches things without expression. Then one time, I was called the "Guy Gnome" because I was doing the same thing. That was the last time I did Ecstasy, and I noticed that I hated it. I don't really like hard drugs. All I do now is drink, smoke weed, and take mushrooms—pretty normal. Every year I drop acid or something.[31]

Kirk's reflections then shift to his feelings about himself. He begins by noting that he doesn't "really know who I am at night," and that this is "a confusing time for me right now." He explains: "The real me is sensitive and confused, and trying to get through this harsh time. I think I am going to be seen as the kid who has everything except brains. He has accomplished everything and is leading a good life. At the same time,

---

29. Ibid., 340.
30. Ibid., 340.
31. Ibid., 340–41.

he's not very happy with things. He's depressed sometimes. There is definitely always something going on inside. I'm confused. I'm not happy."[32]

He notes that growing up in the year 2000 is hard and definitely so "for a guy." Going through high school is tough, and there are a lot of pressures: "I have pressures in sports, school, life all rolled into one. My parents pressure me to do well in school, do well in sports, and I pressure myself to do well in life. My sister got like 4.0 GPA and 1450 on her SATs. She didn't party at all in high school. We are exact opposites. It's so hard to live up to her that I never really tried."[33]

Kirk has always been "a huge athlete" but "not great in school." The primary reason for the latter is that he has documented "learning disabilities." He explains:

> Slow processing, poor concentration, but I don't have dyslexia or anything. I definitely do have some minor disability. It's hard sometimes, especially here in school. I've got something the other kids don't, and they have something I don't have. I blame it on an accident I had. I almost drowned as a child, as a baby. I was at the bottom of our pool for two minutes before my mom found me and gave me CPR. The doctors said nothing happened, but I personally disagree. I think I was damaged.[34]

He goes on to say that he feels misunderstood because everyone tells him that he is smart. He doesn't think this is true, but in the past, "I used to get down on myself a lot," thinking that he was somehow to blame. Also, "as much as my parents would say to me 'Don't ever let anyone say you're stupid' it only made me start to think that I was stupid. I told them that if they were trying to help, it wasn't working. I remember being teased back then, too, and getting upset about being made fun of. I was always a really good athlete and good with the girls. But kids knew where and how to attack me. They all knew that I wasn't the smartest kid in class."[35]

Kirk concludes these self-reflections on a note of uncertainty: "I worry about life a lot. I feel like everything is going to work out for everybody except me, that I'll be left behind in the dust. But I think everything will come together. I'll be on my own, learning to live."[36]

32. Ibid., 341.
33. Ibid.
34. Ibid.
35. Ibid.
36. Ibid.

Unlike Francis, who is looking toward the future with considerable confidence, Kirk worries that he will be "left behind in the dust." He seems to have good reason to feel this way. Whereas Francis says he doesn't go to school thinking, "Oh, God, I have to get into a top college so I can fill my dad's shoes," Kirk has had doubts whether he would get into any college. He is relieved that he did get accepted, but he doesn't seem to be all that excited about having gotten accepted. In fact, his acceptance has allowed him to "slack off" a bit.

He also believes that he has a learning disability and says that this has, in fact, been documented. This disability helps to explain why he tends to fall behind the others in class. But no one seems willing, especially his parents, to acknowledge that he does have a learning disability. One possible reason for this denial could be that they, especially his mother, feel guilty over the fact that he almost drowned in the pool when he was a baby.

Readers of this interview might feel that, although he attributes his difficulties in school to a learning disability, Kirk should instead attribute them to his substance abuse. I believe, however, that the drug abuse may have been a way of giving his brain a break because thinking is very hard work for him. The problem is that the next day he feels "retarded," and his body feels "like a piece of shit."[37] The very word "retarded," which is commonly used in reference to mental deficiencies, suggests that his *straggler* identity has everything to do with his mental capacities. His comparison of himself with his sister focuses on her mental abilities as represented in her grades and SAT scores. We saw in the case of Michael, presented in the preceding chapter on the *stumbler*, that his sister was a hard act to follow because she was not only "really smart, a good student, and did well in math," but also "a big athlete and sports star at school." He says that his parents expect him to "be better" than Sarah. His observation that this is "kind of hard to do" is something of an understatement.[38]

The difficulty that Kirk faces in this regard is that his sister's achievements were more narrowly focused on her scholastic work, and this very focus makes his difficulties in this regard stand out even more. As he points out, "She didn't party at all in high school," and adds, "We are exact opposites." There are many cases where siblings who are "exact opposites" are not subject to invidious comparisons because one, for ex-

37. Ibid., 340.
38. Ibid., 156.

ample, excels in the sciences and the other excels in the arts. This is not the case here. A high school student who excels at partying is unlikely to receive an award for this ability on graduation day.

Kirk is aware that he could never compete with his sister. He says, "It's so hard to live up to her that I never really tried." But this was not merely because he was lazy or lacked motivation. He knows that he has a learning disability even if it is difficult for others to detect. I see no reason to doubt the accuracy of this self-assessment. He is aware that he processes information more slowly than the other students do, and that his concentration is also poor in comparison with theirs. The fact that he has been the object of teasing by other classmates is clear evidence of this fact. His perception that it doesn't help to tell him that he isn't stupid is an especially important insight into how others often relate to the *straggler*. Instead of allowing the *straggler* to proceed at his own pace, they say encouraging things designed to help him quicken his pace and to try to keep up with the others.

In this regard, Thoreau's comment in the concluding chapter of *Walden* is truly a word of grace: "If a man does not keep pace with his companions, perhaps it is because he hears a different drummer. Let him step to the music which he hears, however measured or far away. It is not important that he should mature as soon as an apple-tree or an oak. Shall he turn his spring into summer?"[39] On the other hand, Thoreau's reference to a person's companions raises an issue that seems to be a concern of Kirk's. Although Kirk has friends, is a good athlete, and is able to relate well with the girls, he does not seem to believe that these qualities will offset the fact that he is by no means "the smartest kid in class." Nor does he seem to view them as resources on which to draw in his struggle not to be "left behind in the dust." Perhaps he believes that his friends will not be there for him as he proceeds at his own pace and, as a consequence, falls behind. Will anyone hang back from the others so that he is not left all alone? Will being a good athlete matter as much in college as it does in high school as a means of maintaining friendships? And will his ability to relate to girls count for much as they seek out boys who have a more promising future ahead of them?

There is, in other words, a sense of loneliness that pervades Kirk's account of his life and anticipated future. In fact, Pollack titles the interview "Alone." And, as he also observes in his general description of

39. Thoreau, *Walden*, 255.

the boys who are the subjects of his chapter on addictions, "many of them speak of a painful sense that no one really knows or understands who they really are, that no one cares about their true, inner lives, that they may never find friends with whom they can connect in a genuine, loving way."[40]

Kirk feels that there is, in fact, a "real me" who is unknown to others and sometimes inaccessible to himself. As he puts it, "I don't really know who I am when I'm alone at night. It's a confusing time for me right now. The real me is sensitive and confused, and trying to get through this harsh time."[41] In order to know himself, he needs to be known by another, and this, I believe, is what makes Kirk's journey a fundamentally religious one. Albert Schweitzer concludes *The Quest of the Historical Jesus* with these words:

> He comes to us as One unknown, without a name, as of old, by the lake-side, he came to those men who knew him not. He speaks to us the same word: "Follow thou me!" and sets us to the tasks that He has to fulfill for our time. He commands. And to those who obey, whether they be wise or simple, He will reveal himself in the toils, the conflicts, the sufferings that they shall pass through in his fellowship, and, as an ineffable mystery, they shall learn in their own experience Who He is.[42]

---

40. Pollack, *Real Boys' Voices*, 326.

41. Ibid., 341.

42. Schweitzer, *The Quest of the Historical Jesus*, 403. Schweitzer himself may be viewed as something of a *straggler*. In his *Memoirs of Childhood and Youth* he relates that when he was about eleven or twelve years old he "was not a good student." The reason was that he was "too much given to day-dreaming," adding: "My bad report cards caused my parents much sorrow, yet I did not find the energy to pull myself together and do better" (48). He relates how his father was summoned to see the school principal, who hinted that it might be best to take his son out of school because he was in danger of losing the scholarship he had as a pastor's son. Until this happened, Albert, in his dreaminess, did not fully appreciate the worries that he was causing his father. But his father did not scold him—"he was too kind and too sad for that"—and just "at that juncture a savior appeared in the person of a new home-room teacher," Dr. Wehmann, who "carefully prepared each class" and "knew exactly how much ground he wanted to cover in it and always completed what he planned" (49). He also "returned tests punctually on the due date and in the due hour" (49). Schweitzer notes: "This self-discipline which I observed in him had an influence on me. I would have been ashamed to displease this teacher. He became my model" (49). His grades improved, and he continued to visit Dr. Wehmann after the teacher was transferred to other towns and cities.

Perhaps, too, Kirk will come to know who he himself is as he comes to know the identity of the stranger—the One unknown—by fulfilling tasks He has set for him. Also, considering the fact that Pollack titles the interview "Alone," it is significant that Jesus called the men he encountered by the lake his "friends" because they respond to his commands and he confides in them: "You are my friends if you do what I command you. I do not call you servants any longer, because the servant does not know what the master is doing; but I have called you friends, because I have made known to you everything that I have heard from my Father" (John 15:14–15).

Facing the prospect of being left behind by his friends as they strike out on their respective journeys, Kirk does not need to be friendless. In fact, he could not ask for a better, more faithful friend than Jesus himself. Joseph M. Scriven, an Irishman who immigrated to Canada when he was twenty-five years old, exclaimed in a poem titled *Pray without Ceasing* (1869): "What a friend we have in Jesus." He went on to ask, "Can we find a friend so faithful who will all our sorrows share?" The implied answer is, of course, no. In fact, he goes on to say that if you are despised or forsaken by your friends, you can pray to Jesus about this, and he, the truly faithful friend, will shield you in his arms and console you. This poem was set to music a few years later by Charles C. Converse, an American lawyer and composer, and is one of our most cherished hymns.[43]

Kirk concludes the interview on a cautious note of confidence. Although he worries about life a lot and feels like everything is going to work out for everybody except him, that he will be left behind in the dust, he also thinks "everything will come together" and that perhaps something positive will come from the fact that he will "be on my own, learning to live." The others, if they take the trouble to look back, will think that he is all alone. But if his traveling companion is Jesus, they will be none the wiser, and Kirk may well be secretly gloating, "Maybe I'm not as stupid as they think. In fact, I just might be the smartest kid in class."

43. Scriven immigrated to Canada shortly after his fiancé drowned the night before they were to be married. In Canada he fell in love again and was planning to get married but his fiancé suddenly fell ill of tuberculosis. His poem, written in 1869, was written shortly after the death of one of his fiancés. He himself drowned (at the age of sixty-seven) when he became critically ill and, in a delirious state, got out of bed, went outdoors and fell into a creek. (Online: http://christianmusic.suite101.com/article.cfm/what_a_friend_we_have_in_jesus; http://en.wikipedia.org/wiki/Joseph_M_Scriven.

Mikko: The Curative Suicide Attempt

In a chapter titled "Problems as Friends" in *Solution Talk*, Ben Furman tells about a counseling session that began with a telephone call he received from a woman who was worried about her nephew.[44] She wanted to make him an appointment for a consultation with Furman. She said that Mikko, her nephew, was a high school student who had been doing fine until a month ago when without any warning he made an attempt to kill himself by taking an overdose of sleeping pills. He had been rushed to the hospital, kept overnight, and released the following day. His suicide attempt had come as a terrible shock to everyone in the family.

During the telephone conversation, Furman also learned that a few months prior to his suicide attempt Mikko had been informed that the man he knew as his father was in fact his stepfather. After asking for and receiving information about his biological father, Mikko had called him and they agreed to meet. The encounter, however, was brief and it was clear to Mikko that his biological father was not interested in any further contact. This series of events, together with the fact that he was heavily burdened by his high school studies, was thought by the family to have triggered his suicide attempt.

When Mikko came to Furman's office, he began by talking openly and confidently about how he had been busy the past month with his studies and that he also had a steady girlfriend. The events that had happened a few weeks earlier seemed to belong to the past. When Furman summarized his conversation with Mikko's aunt, Mikko told him the details of his suicide attempt. From his description of the night he tried to kill himself, Furman got a clear impression that he really did try to take his life even though the quantity of the tranquilizers he had swallowed was insufficient to kill him. He also talked about his previous encounter with his father, and about the fact that his father did not seem interested in maintaining contact. But in contrast to his family, who believed the causes of his suicide attempt were the revelation about the man he thought was his father not being his father after all and his father's lack of interest in further meetings, Mikko said this simply wasn't true.

Furman said he was interested in hearing Mikko's own explanation if he wanted to tell him. Mikko told him that when he was in his first few years at primary school, he had a good friend, Jolle. The two boys

---

44. Furman and Ahola, *Solution Talk*, 148–51.

were almost glued to each other. One day, for no apparent reason, Jolle abandoned Mikko and started to play with other boys instead: "This incident broke Mikko's heart. He came to believe that there must be something wrong with him even if he could not figure out what it was. Mikko never spoke about his misery to anyone and he secretly started to harbor thoughts of self-reproach and suicide. The memory of his rejection and the plans for killing himself had stayed with Mikko throughout the years. According to him, the suicide attempt was not precipitated by his current circumstances as the family seemed to think, but was the completion of a private plan he had kept hidden for years."[45]

Furman asked him, "What now, after your suicide attempt?" Specifically, has he spoken about these things to his family? Mikko replied, "I have spoken with my father more than ever." (The fact that he referred to his stepfather as his father is noteworthy in light of the recent revelation that this man was not his biological father.) Furman said, "So, he now knows all about Jolle and the suicidal thoughts that you used to have but kept secret from everyone?"

Mikko replied, "Yes," and added that besides speaking with his father he had also talked with his mother and his girlfriend about many things he had previously kept inside.[46]

Furman concluded that Mikko's suicide attempt had acted as a rite of passage: "A formerly reserved young man who used to conceal his tormenting thoughts and feelings had become able to open up his heart to those close to him."[47] He said to Mikko:

> This may sound odd to you, but in a sense we could say that these events—your overdose and its aftermath—have changed you. You used to keep important thoughts and feelings inside yourself but your suicide attempt has helped you to somehow unlock your ability to talk. After recovering from your overdose you spoke of your intentions and while doing this you realized that you could actually talk about anything. The problem of keeping things to yourself seems to have dissolved as you now feel able to say to others whatever it is you need to tell them. What do you think? Is this true?[48]

---

45. Ibid., 149.
46. Ibid.
47. Ibid., 150.
48. Ibid.

Mikko agreed that it was true. They talked further about how after the suicide attempt he had in many ways become more mature as a person.

Following this discussion, Furman observed that he was in a slightly complicated situation. He noted that Mikko's family may think that he needs psychotherapy, but it now appears that his suicide attempt has, in a sense, cured him. He asked Mikko how his parents would react to this idea. Mikko said he believed that they would agree because, after all, he had spoken so much with them lately.

Furman then asked about his aunt. If Mikko were to present this interpretation to her, would she feel that Furman was not taking his case seriously enough? Mikko replied that he could explain it to her, and that he believed she too would understand. Furman said that in light of what had transpired during the session, he did not think there was a need for psychotherapy. He thanked Mikko for an interesting discussion and walked him to the door. As Mikko was leaving, he said that he could call him any time if he needed his help and wished him well with his studies.

It was only after the session that Furman began to have second thoughts. Was his view that Mikko's suicide attempt had been a self-cure appropriate, or had he simply been too eager to make the therapy brief? He suspected that many of his colleagues would disapprove, but he somehow felt he had done the right thing. He followed up on the case a month later and then again after a year. He learned that Mikko's parents had at first been doubtful about his decision not to recommend further therapy but had, in time, become more confident that it was the right decision as they observed that Mikko did well in his studies, had many friends, and appeared, in his mother's words, to be "a sunny boy."[49]

I have presented this case in this chapter on the *straggler* (despite the fact that it is similar in many respects to the case of Michael presented in the chapter on the *struggler*) because it involved a situation in which a teenage boy was unable to move forward because of an experience that had happened many years earlier. It was not so much a case of a boy having fallen behind the others who were out ahead of him, but of a boy who was unable to keep pace with his own desires and aspirations because something inside him was pulling and dragging him back. His suicide attempt enabled him to shed this internal burden and to move confidently forward on the journey of life. He had lost a cherished friend in the primary grades and had ever since been harboring feelings of self-

---

49. Ibid., 151.

reproach and thoughts about ending his life. But as the chapter title—"Problems as Friends"—indicates, he found a new friend, as it were, in the problem itself. He tried to end his life but was unsuccessful. He now knew that he would never again try to act on the thought of ending his life. In fact, the thought itself had been expelled from his mind.

An important aspect of the cure was that he was able to tell his parents that the revelation involving his father was not the reason he tried to commit suicide. In a sense, the reason was far more personal than this. He had suddenly lost a cherished friend and did not understand why. We can well imagine that his parents were enormously relieved that their own actions (the circumstances relating to his paternity and their failure to disclose the truth about it earlier) was not responsible for his suicide attempt. Also, their disclosure may have played some role in his capacity to disclose his own thoughts and feelings to them.

Still, the suicide attempt itself was the catalytic factor in Mikko's new capacity to talk about his thoughts and feelings to others. It is noteworthy in this regard that Furman suggested to Mikko that he had become "more mature as a person" as a result of the suicide attempt. This maturity is reflected in his ability to talk more openly not only with his parents but also with his steady girl friend. In fact, his relationship with his girlfriend is likely to be the primary beneficiary of the maturity he has gained as a result of his suicide attempt because it is not unlikely that his fears of abandonment by a cherished friend had been rekindled when he began to become seriously involved with this new friend.

Finally, it is possible that the encounter with his biological father *did* have something to do with the fact that his suicide attempt occurred when it did. After all, his father did to him what his friend Jolle had done to him years earlier by indicating that he really didn't want to have anything more to do with him. This may well have aroused similar feelings of self-reproach: "Is there something about me that turns others off?" This does not mean, of course, that his explanation for the suicide attempt is not the primary one. It simply means that the explanation that his family had adopted actually supports, in an indirect sort of way, the real explanation.

This chapter began with the case of Henry David Thoreau, a man for whom the *straggler* was a self-chosen identity. As he writes in the concluding chapter of *Walden*: "I love to weigh, to settle, to gravitate toward that which most strongly and rightfully attracts me;—not hang by the beam of the scale and try to weigh less,—not suppose a case, but take the case that is; to travel the only path I can, and that of which no power can resist me."⁵⁰ Thoreau made a virtue of *not* trying to keep up with this "restless, nervous, bustling, trivial Nineteenth Century." Instead, he wanted only "to come to my bearings,—not walk in procession with pomp and parade, in a conspicuous place, but to walk even with the Builder of the universe, if I may."⁵¹ He understood that his very refusal to keep up was the reflection of the fact that the religious quest of the individual, although solitary, is also the audacious bid that a person makes "to bind himself to creation and to the Creator."⁵² For Thoreau, the Creator is no more interested than he is in keeping up with the pace of society. The two of them walk side by side.

Thoreau makes clear that there is no shame in being a *straggler*. On the other hand, we have also seen in the cases presented here that the role of the *straggler* may not be a self-chosen one. One may have become a straggler due to constitutional factors or traumatic experiences over which one has little if any control. Kirk seems prepared to accept the fact that he may have no other choice than to proceed at a slower pace than the others. Mikko seems to have overcome, through an attempt to end his life, the impediment to his ability to move forward with the others. What makes Thoreau's self-chosen role as the *straggler* an important testimony is that it teaches us not to assume that Kirk's future is inherently less hopeful than Mikko's. Kirk, in fact, thinks that "everything will come together."⁵³ Because we share Thoreau's conviction that the Builder of the universe is not ashamed to walk alongside the stragglers of this world, we have every reason to believe that Kirk is right. As noted earlier, however, his journey will seem a less lonely one if he knows in his heart and in his mind that the Builder of the universe is manifestly present in the friend we have in Jesus. Things have a way of coming together when a boy knows that Jesus—who is the way, the truth and the life (John 14:6)—is walking beside him.

---

50. Thoreau, *Walden*, 258.
51. Ibid., 258.
52. Allport, *The Individual and His Religion*, 142.
53. Pollack, *Real Boys' Voices*, 341.

4
The Straddler

IN THE INTRODUCTION I noted that the *straddler* is a person who takes or appears to take both sides of an issue or refuses to commit himself to one side or another. I also noted that *straddling* has a physiological meaning, of placing oneself with each leg on either side of a chair, bench, post, or some other object. I suggested that this experience is relevant to teenage boys because this is a period in life when a boy is often unsure of what he thinks or believes, or has come to believe what he is not supposed to believe. He may therefore remain noncommittal or keep his thoughts to himself even as he is being encouraged by other teenagers and adults to take a stand. If he does take a stand, he may do so with such intensity that he knows he is trying to convince himself that what he is affirming is right or true, or to impress adults with his sense of conviction. I also noted that the *straddler* may find that some issues are more complex than he or others may realize, and it is therefore wise to straddle these issues rather than to try to settle them prematurely.

The physiological meaning of *straddling* ties the theme of the *straddler* to the idea that the teenage boy is striking out on a religious journey, for during a journey one is likely to stop on occasion and sit down and rest. He may at that time take stock of how far he has come and of the distance between where he is now and where he started. His posture—a leg on either side of a bench, a rock, or a tree stump—may symbolize the distance, and the possible difficulties of reconciling the two locations in his mind.

In focusing on the *straddler* in this chapter I hope to make the case that *straddling* can be a good thing. I also hope to show that *straddling* can be a productive way to deal not only with conceptual issues but also with social and interpersonal connections. On the other hand, these very social and interpersonal connections may have conceptual implications. This being the case, a discussion of the teenage *straddler* will necessarily be concerned with the boy's ways of thinking and, more specifically, with the fact that he is developing the capacity to think independently.

Thinking for Oneself

In his chapter in *The Individual and His Religion* on the religion of youth, Gordon W. Allport notes: "Usually it is not until the stress of puberty that serious reverses occur in the evolution of the religious sentiment. At this period of development the youth is compelled to transform his religious attitudes—indeed all his attitudes—from second-hand fittings to first-hand fittings of his personality. He can no longer let his parents do his thinking for him. Although in some cases the transition is fluent and imperceptible, more often there is a period of rebellion."[1]

He cites studies showing that for approximately two-thirds of all youth there is a reaction against parental and cultural teaching, that approximately half of these reactions occur before age sixteen and half later, and that they take many different forms: "Sometimes the youth simply shifts his allegiance to a religious institution different from his parents'. Or he may reach a satisfying rationalism from which religious considerations are forever after eliminated. Sometimes, when the first shadows of doubt appear, he gives up the whole problem and drifts into the style of life, said to be characteristic of modern youth, of opportunism and hedonism. Occasionally the storm arises not because of intellectual doubts, but because of a gnawing sense of guilt and shame, due perhaps to sex conflicts."[2]

Allport's book was published sixty years ago, but what he says about the "reaction" that occurs in adolescence and the forms that it takes are relevant today. So too is his observation that this may also be a period of "religious awakening."

---

1. Allport, *The Individual and His Religion*, 32.
2. Ibid., 33.

He cites a study of college students that he and two other psychologists conducted after World War II that showed that three forms of religious awakening can be identified. (Although some of these students would have been in their early twenties, they were all being asked to report on earlier experiences, and these, we may assume, were largely experiences that occurred during the teenage years.) One is the *definite crisis* (sometimes referred to as a conversion experience). Another is the *emotional stimulus* type of awakening in which the upheaval is slight or absent but the youth is able to designate some single event that served as an affective stimulus to his religious reorientation. A third is a *gradual awakening*, with no specifiable occasion being decisive. About 70 percent of the students reported the third type of awakening, and the remaining 30 percent were almost equally divided between the first and second types.[3]

He notes that where there has been some marked turn or vivid experience there are usually consequences of a lasting and often permanent order. To be sure, backslidings may occur, but this is to be expected following any strenuous moral experience. More important, "the significance of the definite crisis or emotional stimulus lies in the hunger it arouses, and in the charting of a direction of search for appeasing this hunger. Almost always the individual who has once experienced a vividly religious state of mind seeks throughout his life to recapture its inspiration."[4] Thus, for those who have experienced a vividly religious state of mind, this is not the end, but only the beginning, of their search.

Allport also points out that the self-related stories of adolescent religious experience are extraordinarily diverse: "Some youths find that religious conviction flares into being overnight; they are amazed to discover that it has taken so violent a hold upon them. Some report the solemn impression made by confirmation or by first communion. Many linger on the dark side of things, and report that for them the religious sentiment is always pensive. Many, perhaps most, experience wavering faith, with peaks of exaltation and troughs of despair."[5]

He adds that the feeling of alienation from parent and church is common. Also, where the younger child's religious sentiment tended to be more animistic (for example, evolving his religious concepts in con-

3. Ibid., 34.
4. Ibid.
5. Ibid., 34.

nection with electric storms, a time when fear and helplessness are combined with a sensory manifestation of power), the teenager's religious sentiment becomes more moralistic: "Moral judgments are often harsh and positive, whether directed toward others or toward oneself. The adolescent is often a moral absolutist and believes that a God must exist in order to guarantee the moral values to which he holds. Bereavements and suffering call attention to evil and injustice, and often kindle flames of consuming doubt, or else encourage the religious urge, and hasten the development of a religious solution to the problem of evil."[6]

Thus, moral considerations often play a major role in the teenager's transition from second-hand to firsthand fittings to his personality, and his emerging attention to evil and injustice can take contradictory forms, either of moral absolutism or of consuming doubt. Some teenagers may come down heavily on one side or the other while others may vacillate between them. The latter, I suggest, are the *straddlers.*

Allport also notes that as the religious sentiment grows, it overlaps and blends with other sentiments. For example, the teenager who falls in love "finds that the exalted selflessness of this state is not unlike the mystical experience he may have in his religious moments." Or, "romantic ideals of accomplishment may occupy his mind, and his ambition may merge with a religious longing to embrace the whole universe." For some teenagers, art, music or poetry may become a consuming interest, and these may become the avenues through which their religious sentiment comes to fuller expression. We should not find these associations surprising, for "intense feelings always overflow the boundaries of single sentiments and saturate the personality in all its regions."[7]

Allport concludes his discussion of the religion of adolescents with the observation that perhaps the most significant cultural influence on religious development is the fact that youth are normally encouraged to question authority, "to scrutinize critically all established ways of looking at things." It is not necessarily the case that such questioning has the intention of undermining the authority of parents and the church in which one was raised. There is, however, a strong cultural emphasis on the importance of becoming an independent adult who "is ex-

---

6. Ibid., 34–35.
7. Ibid., 35.

pected to outstrip his parents in occupational, social, and educational accomplishments."[8]

Thus, the questioning of authority may have a personal dimension—a personal need to break away from domineering or suffocating parents or from such a church environment—but this personal dimension is likely to be subordinate to the larger social expectation that children will go further in life than their parents were able to go. As we saw in the case of Augustine in chapter 1, his parents had very high ambitions for him—higher, it would appear, than his own aspirations; and looking back, he feels that these ambitions were rather misguided. An irony that Allport does not discuss is the fact that parents are often numbered among those who want their children to succeed beyond what they themselves have accomplished, and yet in order to succeed in this regard their teenage son or daughter will necessarily need to question their parents' ways of looking at things.

Paul Tillich: The Disposition and Tensions of a Straddler

Paul Tillich, the well known Protestant theologian, provides some invaluable insights into the experience of being a *straddler* in his intellectual autobiography titled *On the Boundary*.[9] He begins the autobiography with a reference to his earlier book titled *Religious Realization,* in which he claimed that "the boundary is the best place for acquiring knowledge." When he was asked to write an account of the ways his ideas had developed from his personal life, he remembered what he had said about the boundary and felt "that the concept of the boundary might be the fitting symbol for the whole of my personal and intellectual development."[10] He continues: "At almost every point, I have had to stand between alternative possibilities of existence, to be completely at home in neither and to take no definitive stand against either. Since thinking presupposes receptiveness to new possibilities, this position is fruitful for thought; but it is difficult and dangerous in life, which again and again demands decisions and thus the exclusion of alternatives. This disposition and its tensions have determined both my destiny and my work."[11]

8. Ibid., 36.
9. Tillich, *On the Boundary.*
10. Ibid., 13.
11. Ibid.

This is the description of a *straddler*, and what makes it remarkable is that the writer is very much aware of the fact that he is a *straddler* by nature, and also aware of its strengths but also its difficulties.

Following this brief statement about how he views himself, Tillich proceeds to discuss twelve aspects of his life in which he has maintained the role of the *straddler*. Thus, there are sections (too short to be called chapters) titled "Between Two Temperaments," "Between City and Country," "Between Social Classes," "Between Reality and Imagination," "Between Theory and Practice," "Between Heteronomy and Autonomy," "Between Theology and Philosophy," "Between Church and Society," "Between Religion and Culture," "Between Lutheranism and Socialism," "Between Idealism and Marxism," and "Between Native and Alien Land."

Tillich was born in Prussia in 1886. The first version of his autobiography was published in 1936 when he was fifty years old. An expanded version was published in 1964, and reflects the fact that he was now living in America, an alien land. Several of the book's themes concern polarities that emerged in his adult life, but the majority were present in his teenage years. The first section on temperament focuses on parental and ancestral traits, and notes that his father was from eastern Germany and his mother was from western Germany. He notes that the "inclination to meditation tinged with melancholy, a heightened consciousness of duty and personal sin, and a strong regard for authority and feudal traditions" of eastern Germany was still alive when he was growing up, and that it contrasted with the western German temperament of a "zest for life, love of the concrete, mobility, rationality and democracy."[12] Precisely because his father's influence was dominant, in part because of his mother's early death, the character of his mother's world "asserted itself only through constant and deep struggle with that of my father," and in order for "the maternal side of my makeup to express itself, outbreaks, often extreme, were necessary." This tension, he believes, is reflected in his theory of dynamic truth, "which holds that truth is found in the midst of struggle and destiny, and not, as Plato taught, in an unchanging 'beyond.'"[13]

Tillich also discusses the fact that he lived in a rural environment from four to fourteen years of age, and that his visits to Berlin created a tension in him between his love for the land and his appreciation for the "fantastic inner activity" of the city. But weeks spent by the sea every

12. Ibid., 14.
13. Ibid., 15.

year from the time he was eight years old were even more important for his life and work because the "experience of the infinite bordering on the finite suited my inclination toward the boundary situation and supplied my imagination with a symbol that gave substance to my emotions and creativity to my thought."[14]

The fact that he grew up in a small town made the boundary between social classes visible to him at an early age. He attended public school, made friends there, and shared their animosity toward the upper classes represented by his parents and the families of the mayor, the doctor, the druggist, some merchants, and a few others. He took private lessons in Latin with some of the children of this select group, and he later attended the *Gymnasium* in a nearby city with them, but "my real friends were the boys of the public school," and "this led to a great deal of tension with the children of my own social level, and we remained strangers throughout our schooldays."[15]

He suggests that when a sensitive upper-class child has an early and intimate encounter with children of the lower classes, one of two possible outcomes will occur: the development of a consciousness of social guilt or feelings of class hatred in response to the lower-class children's aggressive resentment. He developed a deep sense of social guilt. On the other hand, his father was a minister, and many of his church's members were from the old landed nobility. His parents had professional and social contact with them, and he was proud that he could visit their manor houses and play with their children. A descendent of one of these families had been his lifelong friend. He believed that his "borderline situation" accounted for the fact that he had attempted to incorporate into his socialism those elements of the feudal tradition that have an inner affinity with the socialist principle.

Another tension that Tillich experienced emerged out of his difficulties in "coming to terms with reality."[16] These difficulties occurred between the age of fourteen and seventeen. He does not say what they were, but they undoubtedly had to do with the fact that the family moved to Berlin in 1900 when he was fourteen years old, because his father had been transferred there; and that his mother died of cancer in 1903 when he was seventeen years old. During these years he "withdrew as often as

14. Ibid., 18.
15. Ibid., 19.
16. Ibid., 24.

possible into imaginary worlds which seemed to be truer than the world outside."[17] He believes that his inclination toward the imaginative has been good in that it has enabled him to combine categories, to perceive abstractions in concrete terms (almost "in color"), and to experiment with a wide range of conceptual possibilities. But it has been of doubtful value in the sense that it runs the risk of mistaking imaginative creations for realities and thus neglecting experience and rational critique. It also tends to isolate a person and to cause him to be less interested in cooperative scientific efforts. He believes, however, that imagination enabled him to engage in games and in sports without taking them too seriously, and as time went on he became especially interested in art because it provided a refuge from the horror, ugliness and destructiveness of war.

An especially difficult issue for him was the tension between heteronomy and autonomy. The issue of the adolescent's questioning of authority (including parental authority) that Allport discusses was particularly problematic for Tillich. Here is how he begins the section on heteronomy and autonomy: "I was able to reach intellectual and moral autonomy only after a severe struggle. My father's authority, which was both personal and intellectual and which, because of his position in the church, I identified with the religious authority of revelation, made every attempt at autonomous thinking an act of religious daring and connected criticism of authority with a sense of guilt. The age-old experience of mankind, that new knowledge can be won only by breaking a taboo and that all autonomous thinking is accompanied by a consciousness of guilt, is a fundamental experience of my own life."[18]

He adds that every theological, ethical, and political criticism that he advanced against the established tradition "encountered inner obstacles that were overcome only after lengthy struggles." But the very fact that so much struggle was involved meant that "the significance, seriousness, and weight of such insights" was greatly heightened.[19] It also means that he does not have any desire to resolve the tension between heteronomy and autonomy by endorsing a pure autonomy, for this is likely to result in a new heteronomy, one that is as problematic as the one it replaces.

17. Ibid.
18. Ibid., 36–37.
19. Ibid., 37.

In the brief concluding section of the autobiography titled "Retrospect: Boundary and Limitation," Tillich notes that although he has written about "many possibilities of human existence," there are many others that have not been mentioned even though they are part of his life story. But each possibility that he *has* discussed has been considered "in its relationship to another possibility—the way they are opposed, the way they can be correlated."[20]

He suggests that this is "the dialectic of existence," that each of life's possibilities drives of its own accord to a boundary and beyond the boundary where it meets that which limits it. Thus, "the man who stands on many boundaries experiences the unrest, insecurity, and inner limitation of existence in many forms. He knows the impossibility of attaining serenity, security, and perfection. This holds true in life as well as in thought, and may explain why the experiences and ideas which I have recounted are rather fragmentary and tentative."[21] He concludes that these limits to human possibilities point to the Eternal, which transcends all human possibilities. On this side of the Eternal, however, a life of *straddling* is perhaps the best that one can do.

Tillich's autobiography is especially relevant to our concern here with the teenage boy because although some of the tensions in his life were present long before he became a teenager, those that caused the more severe struggles emerged in his teenage years. Especially significant in this regard were struggles relating to social class, to the conflict between reality and imagination, and the conflict between heteronomy and autonomy, especially in connection with religious authority. The fact that his father was a minister made the last conflict a more personal one than it might otherwise have been, and this fact is reflected in the fact that this section of the book is much more emotional than the other sections. It is also the section where he is most insistent in his claim that he does not try to resolve the tension between the two polarities or possibilities. In other words, he takes a certain pride in the fact that, in this particular instance, he *was* a *straddler*. In so doing, he lends support to the very idea that straddling is not necessarily a negative thing.

---

20. Ibid., 97.
21. Ibid., 97–98.

Doug: A Seeker for Knowledge

As we have seen, Tillich struggled with social class issues. He did so, however, as a member of the upper class who was sensitive to the disparities between the upper and lower classes as a result of the fact that his best friends were from the lower class. This very sensitivity played a significant role in his conflict between heteronomy and autonomy because heteronomy is a handed-down or even top-down form of authority. We have also noted Gordon Allport's observation that the questioning of authority is tied in with the social expectation that children will go further in life than their parents. This observation is especially relevant to those who have grown up in lower-class families and is supported by a recent study of *straddlers* by Alfred Lubrano.[22] This study focuses on persons who were born into blue-collar families and then moved into the middle class. They are the first in their families to have graduated from college: "As such, they straddle two worlds, many of them not feeling at home in either."[24] Although Lubrano's interviewees included white ethnic and Anglo-Saxon Protestants, African Americans, Hispanics, and Asians, "the members of this demographically disparate group express remarkably similar emotions as they tell strikingly similar tales of the seldom-heard, dark side of mobility."[23]

Lubrano's use of education as the dividing line between working class and middle class fits well with Allport's view that there is a strong relationship between the questioning of authority and education, for a central feature of education is the expectation that one learns to scrutinize critically all established ways of looking at things. Lubrano begins his chapter on the shock of education with this observation: "College is where the great change begins. People start to question the blue-collar take on the world . . . Suddenly, college opens up a world of ideas—a life of the mind—abstract and intangible. The core blue-collar values and goals—loyalty to family and friends, making money, marrying, and procreating—are supplanted by stuff you never talked about at home: personal fulfillment, societal obligation, the pursuit of knowledge for knowledge's sake, and on and on. One world opens and widens; another shrinks."[24]

---

22. Lubrano, *Limbo*.
23. Ibid., 2.
24. Ibid., 47.

Most teenage boys experience the first stirrings of independent thinking while still living at home and before they enter college. But Lubrano expresses well the role that the "life of the mind" plays in the very creation of a *straddler*. As Allport points out, the teenager is beginning to think for himself, and as his account of the various types of religious awakenings indicates, emotions are certainly involved, but the mind is the central locus of the changes that are taking place.

Also, Lubrano implicitly uses the image of a journey in his portrayal of the *straddler*. As he describes it, the world in which there were certainties is fading into the background as one embarks on the road of the pursuit of knowledge, a pursuit that is likely to go on and on. He cites in this connection the comment of a history professor at Southwest Texas State University who mentioned to Lubrano in an interview that he tells all his freshman students, "Every bit of learning takes you further from your parents."[25]

Lubrano also discusses the difficulty that *straddlers* experience in returning home for visits. In his chapter on going home, subtitled "an identity changed forever," he tells about Doug, who grew up in Rock Hill, South Carolina, when it was a small town of 25,000 people.[26] He interviewed Doug and his parents in Rock Hill. After describing Rock Hill, he notes: "Doug never felt comfortable here. And you can see that now, today, in the humid, 95-degree heat. He is jumpy, almost agitated. Memories flood and fill him, a saturation that sets him adrift. Restless, he flits around his parents' living room, a cool, dark place from which the sun is banned like an unwanted intruder."[27]

He notes that there is a painting on the wall that Doug's father painted from memory of the peanut farm in which he had grown up, and adds that Doug's mother also grew up on a farm. They had purchased the small house in which Doug was raised when the area was practically rural. His father worked for years in a factory that made filters for cigarettes until the chemicals in the plant burned his eyes so badly that he quit and started his own construction company.

Doug always felt different from the other kids: "I can't even articulate it. We'd be playing softball in the backyard and I'd be keeping score in my head and they'd make fun of that. They thought it was the weirdest

25. Ibid., 47–48.
26. Ibid., 112–20.
27. Ibid., 112–13.

thing." He was studious and bright, an anomaly among the working class of Rock Hill: "I knew early it was me against the world." Kids teased him until they grew bored with the torture. Too often, he'd be seen reading a book: "That was the stupidest thing in the world to two-thirds of the kids in the class."[28] He tells about the time when another kid knocked him down, pulled a Hardy Boys book from his book bag—*The House on the Cliff*—and kicked it around the schoolyard, scuffing it up.

Doug noticed a difference between his parents and the other adults in town. His parents seemed more intelligent; they were energetic, always thinking, and their number-one goal was to educate their children. Setting a precedent for their part of the town, they spent a substantial portion of his father's take-home pay on encyclopedias for their children. His father had wished he had gotten a chance to go to college, so he made sure that his children understood what was at stake. There were minor conflicts with his father who was a coach of Doug's neighborhood softball team and would have liked to see more effort from his own son, who would rather read than play ball. Years later, Doug turned into a decent player, but his father wasn't coaching then and didn't see the improvement.

Doug found refuge in the library located ten miles from home, to which his mother would drive him so that he could load up on as many books as they would allow him to check out. He recalls reading fairy tales from around the world because he wanted to know what other people were like. He also devoured science fiction, and he read about religion. The religion that prevailed in his hometown did not interest him. He took what he needed from the Bible and rejected what he now calls "that holy roller stuff." He was also drawn to Jewish writers. Philip Roth was a particular favorite.[29] Why would a Christian South Carolina kid fixate on Philip Roth and others? Looking back, Doug thinks this was because "I understood Jewish neurosis." He adds, "I told my wife I think I have a Jewish soul. I'm more intellectual than physical. I see the irony, the comedy in life."[30]

The fact that Winthrop College was in Rock Hill meant that there were middle-class people around and they made the town seem more genteel. Doug was drawn to the campus, with its brick buildings and

28. Ibid., 113.
29. He mentions Roth's *Goodbye Columbus* and *Portnoy's Complaint*.
30. Lubrano, *Limbo*, 115.

quiet elegance. It was a break in the landscape, a kind of garden that didn't seem to belong there.

He also enjoyed talking with his family doctor and his eye doctor: "I had no idea why. They just seemed different, more interesting." He would flirt with girls he liked from his advanced-placement classes, but he wouldn't ask them out on dates because they were doctors' daughters. He was as intelligent as they were, but he felt socially inferior to them because they always seemed so well-dressed and clean: "There was that gulf there. I would have felt very inadequate." He also worked in a local country club one summer and noticed that the members' kids his age were more verbally adroit, more confident. He recalled that they were sneakier and were not as straightforward as he was. In addition, they acted superior. He felt that this was because they were around their parents in social settings and that he and his kind were not. In any event, "Upper-crust kids were just more comfortable talking."[31]

As time went on, he began to feel that Rock Hill had nothing to offer. Guys would drive up and down the main street, showing off cars and trying to pick up girls. He couldn't see himself cruising up and down the same strip year after year: "There's nothing wrong with the people. They're good, honest, try to do the right stuff. But they're not what you'd call generally curious. They don't read; they don't seek knowledge." He added, "I would have preferred to be comfortable there. But I wasn't."[32]

One night he was absentmindedly turning the radio dial one night and he heard a distant station playing Bruce Springsteen's *Born to Run*. He had no idea who the singer was, but he was riveted by the lyrics about escaping the hometown while you are still young: "That really did help focus me. Here was a guy expressing my innermost feelings, feelings in some cases I wasn't even aware of, except in a general anger or resentment."[33] He began to view going to college as the way out and this was, in fact, what his parents had been encouraging all along. His father told Lubrano that he would give Doug onerous chores at home so he wouldn't eschew college like so many of the kids in the neighborhood were doing.

Doug's dream was to go to Duke University, but it was too expensive for his parents to afford, so he went to Clemson, which was closer

31. Ibid., 116.
32. Ibid., 117.
33. Ibid.

to home. His father steered him toward engineering in the belief that engineers run the world, and Doug complied. But he did not know much about engineering, and had no mentors to ask whether he should be studying electrical or chemical engineering. So, as Lubrano puts it, "he stumbled ahead on his own."[34] One semester he took a break from engineering and took courses in liberal arts and won writing awards for his short stories. But he graduated in engineering and went on to do an MBA at Duke University. He told Lubrano that he had read somewhere that white-collar kids study medicine while blue-collar kids go for something more practical, like engineering, if they ever get to college at all. He also noted that his semester of taking liberal arts courses was "a pride thing." He wanted to prove to himself but also to the middle-class kids in these classes that he, a blue-collar kid, could do it.

But one day during his studies at Duke, the head of the Disney Corporation came to campus for a visit and invited some students, including Doug, to lunch. Doug had the sense that the CEO "was judging how articulate the students were, measuring them for possible employment down the road." Two classmates kept the CEO engrossed and entertained, weaving charming stories that starred themselves, while Doug hardly said anything. He said to Lubrano, "Those upper-crust kids really know how to ingratiate themselves." The CEO never contacted Doug, and, as Lubrano notes, Doug had "tripped over his working-class roots."[35]

Because the focus of his book is the difficulties that persons who grow up in a blue-collar world experience when they enter the world of the middle class, Lubrano emphasizes the fact that Doug straddled two very different social classes. But if we look closely at his life and experiences during his teenage years, social class seems to have been the one area of his life in which he knew he could *not* be a *straddler*. He was very much aware of the fact that he was born into a blue-collar family and there was really no way that he could even presume to straddle the two social classes. If one of his parents had been blue-collar and the other middle class or higher, he may well have felt that he could somehow straddle the class structure of Rock Hill. But he did not attempt to do so. He flirted with doctors' daughters, but he did not ask them out on a date. He worked at the local country club but recognized the

34. Ibid., 117.
35. Ibid., 118.

gulf between himself and the "upper-crust" kids and did not attempt to bridge the gulf.

On the other hand, I believe that he was a *straddler* as defined in the introduction and in the opening sentence of this chapter. That is, his thought processes were those of a *straddler*. This was especially reflected in the fact that, as Lubrano puts it, "the Christianity that flourishes strong and fervent in these parts did not completely germinate in Doug," that he took what he needed from the Bible and discarded the rest, that he read fairy tales from around the world because he wanted to know what other people were like, and that he was attracted to New York Jewish writers because there was something in himself that resonated with their ironic view of life. This was not fundamentally a class issue, for he was engaging in ways of thinking that were just as foreign to the middle and upper classes in Rock Hill as they were to the blue-collar class.

His mother told Lubrano that it was "frightening" when Doug was fourteen years old because she did not know how to handle his "intelligence." She added that he read all the books there were to read, and that "we knew he was special." This caused her to worry that she wouldn't be able to "give him what it would take for him to become what he should become," and she confesses that a few times she thought, "Lord, why can't I have a normal child?"[36] It may be that she felt that a boy with her son's "intelligence" would have been a more "normal" occurrence in a middle-class or upper-middle-class family, but I tend to doubt it. Surely she would have known that not all or even most of the middle-class kids in Rock Hill were highly intelligent. What made her son "abnormal" was not, therefore, that he was born into a blue-collar family, but that he was highly intelligent, and highly intelligent children present their parents with a difficult challenge. To be sure, blue-collar parents would wonder if they could come up with the financial resources for his college education, but this would also be true for most middle-class parents too, especially if they had several children who would be attending college at the same time.

Doug's mother's comments to Lubrano underscore the fact that Doug was a *straddler* in the way his mind worked, in the way he critically scrutinized established ways of looking at things, and, more specifically, in the fact that he viewed the world and perhaps his own place within it from the perspective of irony. In *A Rhetoric of Irony*, Wayne Booth

36. Ibid., 116.

makes a useful distinction between metaphor and irony. He suggests that metaphor tends to be "additive" in that it invites the reader to see in it a plenitude of meanings, whereas irony is "subtractive" in that it tends to discount even those meanings that appear to be true or self-evident. Thus, whereas metaphor invites the conviction that "there is more here than meets the eye," irony creates the suspicion that there is less.[37]

It would not be altogether surprising if an intelligent boy growing up in Rock Hill would come to believe that there is less here than meets the eye. Watching another boy kick one of his books around the schoolyard would support this conclusion, but so would a summer of working at the local country club. As an ironist, he does not aspire to make his way into the middle and upper classes. No, he simply wants out.

There is also something rather "subtractive" about his approach to the Bible, as taking from it what he needs and discarding the rest. Lubrano does not elaborate on what he kept and what he discarded, but I like to imagine that one of the verses he kept was Proverbs 26:17: "He who meddles in a quarrel not his own is like one who takes a passing dog by the ears." I can see Doug listening to the conflicting opinions of blue-collar and upper crust residents of Rock Hill and concluding that this is a quarrel that is not his own. Instead, he will follow the dog to see what the dog is sniffing out, even if—or especially if—this takes him to the highway that leads out of town.

As we have seen, Gordon Allport identifies three forms of religious awakenings that typically occur among teenagers, the definite crisis, the emotional stimulus, and the gradual awakening. Hearing Bruce Springsteen singing "Born to Run" qualifies, it would seem, as the second type of awakening, which Allport goes on to describe as one in which "the upheaval is slight or absent, but wherein, nonetheless, the subject is able to designate some single event which served as the effective stimulus to his religious reorientation." He adds that the emotional stimulus, like the definite crisis, is significant for "the hunger it arouses, and in the charting of a direction of search for appeasing this hunger."[38]

No doubt, few residents of Rock Hill, including his contemporaries and probably Doug himself, would have viewed his experience of being riveted by Springsteen's "Born to Run" as a *religious* awakening. But as Allport also notes, "the religious quest of the individual is solitary" and

37. Booth, *A Rhetoric of Irony*, 177–78.
38. Allport, *The Individual and His Religion*, 34.

is also the region of mental life that has the longest-range intentions."[39] Both are true of Doug's experience. He was alone and bored that night and listening to Springsteen "really did help focus me" because here "was a guy expressing my innermost feelings, feelings in some cases I wasn't even aware of, except in a general anger or resentment."[40]

Thus, what Springsteen's lyrics did for him was to turn these feelings of anger or resentment into intentions, intentions based on the belief that he needed to leave his hometown while he was still young. There may also have been something compelling about the idea that he was *born* to run, that his eventual escape from Rock Hill was there from birth, and that all the intervening years had been preparation for the run itself.

As for what happened to him after he left Rock Hill, he seems to have continued to live out the role—or identity—of the *straddler*. His father wanted him to become an engineer, and based this desire for his son on the belief that engineers run the world. Doug, however, seems to have had an interest in medicine, as reflected in the fact that he liked to sit and talk with doctors when he was a boy and mentioned reading a book that said white-collar kids study medicine while blue-collar kids go for something more practical, like engineering. Medicine is devoted to helping people maintain or regain their health or, as Lubrano points out, to help relieve the permanent pain that is the inevitable outcome of the work life of men like Doug's father. Hence, it too is eminently practical. But Doug may have been suggesting that the process of becoming a doctor is impractical because the years of training to become one are longer and more expensive. In any event, he did not pursue a career in medicine.

But there was also the semester in which he took liberal arts courses. He now says that he did this to prove to himself that he could do it. But given the fact that he was an inveterate reader as a boy, that he was especially interested in novels, and the fact that he also wrote short stories during this semester that won awards, it is altogether likely that there was more to this foray into liberal arts than the simple desire to prove to himself that he could do it. Perhaps he envisioned himself becoming a writer or a professor. In any event, he followed the path that his

39. Ibid., 141–42.
40. Lubrano, *Limbo*, 117.

father wanted him to follow and, as Lubrano points out, "he stumbled ahead on his own."[41]

By seeking to straddle between his father's intentions for him (which were clear) and his own intentions for himself (which were less clear) he became a *stumbler*. But then he was able to go to Duke University after all and to pursue an MBA degree. From there he decided to work for the National Security Agency in Maryland, met his future wife there, and subsequently moved to Austin, Texas, where he became a program manager for a high-tech firm. Did he become his own man?[42] It appears that he did, for as he said to Lubrano in reference to the place where he grew up, "The biggest problem I see with the whole thing [is that] everybody has to be in some pigeonhole, or people aren't comfortable with you."[43]

These are the words of a *straddler,* and *straddling* is a viable way to live one's life. What it lacks in moral conviction is more than made up for in its sense of irony. As an inveterate reader of books would certainly have recognized, irony is itself a sort of pilgrim in the world of literary forms. For, as Booth points out, what makes irony effective is that its meanings are not transparent but hidden within the surface of the text.[44] This means that it becomes an invited (if the irony is intentional) or uninvited (if the irony is unintentional) stranger in whatever text it appears, but that it has no official status there. Its effectiveness in any literary form (novel, short story, play, poem, or essay) depends on its essential *homelessness,* on the fact that, generically speaking, it cannot be tied down and refuses to be domesticated. It is like Doug himself who, as Lubrano observes, is jumpy, almost agitated, as he restlessly flits around his parents' living room, that cool, dark place from which the sun itself is banned like an unwanted intruder.

Also, as D. C. Muecke points out, for many ironists, God is the supreme ironist.[45] If this is so, it means that God is also homeless in the world and derives transcendent freedom from this very homelessness.

41. Ibid., 117.

42. "Becoming One's Own Man" is a phrase that Daniel Levinson employs in *The Seasons of a Man's Life* to apply to men who are in the late "Settling Down" phase (age thirty-six to forty). He suggests that this is the phase in which a man is beginning "to become a senior member in one's profession, to speak more strongly with one's own voice, and to have a greater measure of authority" (60).

43. Lubrano, *Limbo,* 120

44. Booth, *A Rhetoric of Irony,* 6.

45. Muecke, *Irony,* 38.

When Doug's mother tells Lubrano that there were times she asked, "Lord, why can't I have a normal child?" she was perhaps witnessing to the fact that God is the supreme ironist, for God had given her, of all people, a gifted child. And this brings us to one more aspect of Doug's role—or identity—as a *straddler,* namely, the fact that being a son of this father and this mother was itself a *straddling* act. As Doug said to Lubrano, "My dad still thinks I'm a momma's boy because I didn't get under the hood of a car and because I preferred books." Yet, as we have seen, when he left home to go to college, he followed his father's urging that he major in engineering and not in the liberal arts. As far as parental influence was concerned, he did not come down on one side or the other.

Booth contends that every ironist needs to deal with the issue of "learning where to stop." Irony can end in nihilism, but this need not be the case. He recommends, therefore, that the reader look for that place in an ironic text where the irony stops and relinquishes itself to a stable conviction or vision.[46] Booth's point also applies to the supreme ironist, who saw to it that Doug's parents agreed on the importance of a college education and also saw to it that, on this point, Doug shared their common conviction.

John: Religious Doubts

As we saw in the case of Doug, some teenage boys become invested in what he referred to as the search for knowledge. It bothered him that other boys his age were not "generally curious." As far as his religious sentiment was concerned, he read about religion and took from the Bible what he needed and discarded the rest. Our next *straddler* is a teenage boy named John who is having religious doubts, yet has remained active in his church youth group and was recently elected president of the group.[47]

As Robin, the director of Christian education, tells us, John is a high school freshman and the youngest boy in a family of three boys. No one in the family has ever attended the church or shown any interest in his activity there. He had attended church school until he reached seventh grade and then dropped out, but remained active in the youth group. He has always appeared to be an unusually quiet boy but very

---

46. Booth, *A Rhetoric of Irony,* 244.
47. Cryer and Vayhinger, *Casebook in Pastoral Counseling,* 147–52.

cooperative. He has been reluctant to take any place of importance but is always willing to do behind-the-scenes work.

John was on Robin's list of teenagers eligible for church membership classes but when he raised the subject with John at a Sunday evening meeting, John indicated that he was not interested in becoming a church member. So Robin suggested to John that he might come in to talk about it. They agreed to meet the following Saturday morning. Robin did not make any further effort to remind John of their scheduled meeting, so he was rather doubtful that John would remember. But he did remember, and, what's more, he arrived on time.

They went into the church parlor where they could be comfortable while they talked. As they sat down together, John said that he just doesn't want to join the church and, anyway, his parents are Methodists. Robin asked if his parents attended the Methodist church, and John said no, that they don't go to any church, but that his grandfather was the minister of the Methodist church for a long time. He added that even if he were a Methodist, he wouldn't become an official member. Robin said that perhaps being a church member just wasn't all that important to John, to which John replied, "I guess it's important, but, well, I feel uncomfortable in church." When Robin asked if he felt uncomfortable because he doesn't understand the procedures or the sermon John answered:

> No, it's not that. It's not the sermon or anything. It's the whole church. It's funny. I can't really explain it. You know, I wanted to be in the choir but then I have to go to church, and I feel so funny. I did join the choir once. Mr. Gregory says I have a pretty good voice—I guess I must have a pretty fair voice or he wouldn't say that. It can't be so bad. Anyhow, he let me in the choir. Then the first Sunday I went in the church I didn't know what to do, and when the choir went out I just stood there until they were halfway up the aisle before I woke up. Man, I felt silly.[48]

Robin said that he could imagine how embarrassed he must have felt and why he wouldn't want to be in church after an experience like that. But John said this really wasn't the reason he feels so funny in church. He seemed to be on the verge of explaining what the reason was, but then he paused and stared down at his hands.

---

48. Ibid., 148.

Robin asked John if he only felt ill at ease in church, to which John replied, "No, I also feel funny when I have to go up on the stage at school or say something at youth group." Robin commented that perhaps he was afraid people wouldn't approve of him, but John indicated that this wasn't it: "No, I guess people like me well enough—they must, don't you think? Yeah, I guess they like me as well as anyone else. Maybe they even like me better than most kids. They elected me president of the youth group. They must like me some or they wouldn't do that."[49]

Robin responded that it's not that he's afraid of people, then, and John agreed: "I can make myself face people and get up in front of them, but I can't sit in church. I just can't stand to sit there . . . . I can't."[50]

Struggling to understand what John was trying to tell him, Robin asked him if he simply didn't feel that he belonged in church. John replied, "Well, not exactly. I'll bet there are about 30 or 40 per cent of the people who come to church every Sunday who feel just like I do—I mean, who don't believe in God." Robin was taken aback by John's confession, but responded, "So when you're in church you feel like you're being dishonest by being there."

John said:

> That's it. I just can't go to church any more. I can't—I don't—believe in God, and never will. You see, I used to pray all the time. Nobody knew I was praying, but I just always prayed. I never prayed for anything for myself. But like during the war—I wasn't very old but I used to pray hard that the war would end, but it didn't. It didn't, and lots of people were killed and homes were wrecked and . . . well, I prayed for other things too, like when my aunt was in an accident I prayed that she would get well. She wanted to so much. She wanted to be doing her housework and things. I don't know why, but she did. And instead of getting better she got worse. She finally got well but—there just can't be any God. Now just look, there's another war and any day now my two brothers will be going in the army and might be killed. Nobody can make me believe in God.[51]

Trying hard not to get into a theological discussion with John, Robin simply responded by saying that everything makes it look like

49. Ibid., 148.
50. Ibid.
51. Ibid., 149.

there really isn't any God. John said, "It sure does," then added that he likes astronomy and that astronomy makes him think more and more that there isn't any God.

Robin suggested that perhaps coming to the church membership class might help him understand some of these things, but John replied, "It's no use. They always give the same answers, 'God didn't want it that way, that's why your prayers were not answered.' Well, if God wants a war I don't want God." Robin said, "So you don't think there is any answer to your problem," and John responded, "Nope, all these things that are supposed to be proofs of God are just coincidences—that's all."[52]

Robin indicated that he needed to end their conversation at this point but suggested to John that they might talk some more if it helps to talk with someone. John responded by saying that he really dreaded coming here this morning and could hardly make himself come: "Finally it was too late for me even to eat breakfast, but I came because I told you I would. I don't think I want to come back and talk with you, but if I decide to can I tell you at youth group tomorrow night?" Robin said that this was perfectly okay with him, and as John got up to go he said, "So long, see you tomorrow night."[53]

In his comments on this conversation, Robin said that he was very concerned about John but felt very unsure in the situation. He wondered how much one can do with a boy this age without disturbing him further and perhaps making it impossible to continue working with him. He also noted that he had great difficulty in controlling his "desire to respond to his religious problems with intellectual answers," and added that this was the first time he had a conversation with someone who paused so often and was struggling all the time for words. However, Robin felt that such responses would not have been helpful, for John "presents a total picture of insecurity and a strong desire to be dependent upon someone."[54] This prompted Robin to wonder what John's relationship with his brothers and parents is like.

Robin also noted that John commented on his election to the position of president of the youth group and that he feels this indicates group approval. He adds, "I'm not sure I understand why he was elected. I never expected him to be since there were others nominated who are

52. Ibid.
53. Ibid.
54. Ibid., 150.

generally very popular and who really assume leadership in the group. John is accepted but he's not an all-around popular guy."[55]

Sunday evening John was a half hour late to the youth group and during this time Robin was very concerned, thinking he might not show up at all. But the following Sunday he arrived on time and conducted the meeting fairly well but was constantly looking to Robin for direction and consulting with him about many of the business matters that had to be brought up. Nor has he asked to talk further about his religious doubts. On the other hand, Robin felt that their relationship has been warm and has not been at all disturbed by their conversation.

In his comment on the case, Roy A. Burkhart, who had served as a youth director, a former high school principal, and a pastor, suggests that perhaps the youth program could include discussion of some of "the intellectual problems which are related to John's situation," such as why there is war, why is there suffering, and why things happen to hurt people. He thinks that as John observes other teenagers entering into the discussion "he might not only be surprised to find out that they share his feelings and are still devoted to the church, but he might come to new insight and new understanding." He also suggests that it could well be that "the real problem is not John's question about God and about war but, as the director indicated, a deep insecurity," adding, "It may be related to the total family situation which, if understood, would throw light on the boy's feelings."[56]

In his comment on the case, Wayne E. Oates, who was a professor of psychology of religion at a theological seminary at the time, suggests that John is suffering from some "deeper shock" in his meaningful interpersonal relationships, and that he seems to be deflecting this shock to a larger context—the war, his aunt's illness, and his concerns about his brothers going off to war. Oates does not indicate what sort of "deep shock" he has in mind. In fact, he hesitates to speculate as to what it might be, but instead simply states that whatever it may be, "John has been disillusioned, disappointed, and confused by those in whom he has placed confidence." Inasmuch as he views John's "shock" as being even more personal than his concerns about his aunt and his brothers, perhaps he has in mind one or both of John's parents. In any event, he thinks it would be wise for Robin to initiate a careful but unobtrusive

55. Ibid.
56. Ibid., 150–51.

observation of John's family situation, that this would give a larger picture of what is bothering him.[57]

Oates also suggests that John "may be feeling the first flushes of a need to rebel and break away from his parents, his teachers, his church." He notes that John's assertion that "nobody can make me believe there is a God" indicates that he feels he is being coerced, and that his individuality is being threatened: "This creates storm and stress, and his rebellion creates a feeling of isolation and being misunderstood." Oates adds that this rebellion "takes a definite religious direction," and, this being the case, he finds it encouraging because, if it is handled properly, this rebellion "may be a prelude to a more positive revelation of religious reality and certainty."[58]

He also focuses on Robin's role as John's confidante. He suggests that in his concern not to impose his own agenda on John, Robin may have overlooked his own role as a friend to him at a time of transition from his home-dependence to the larger human community. He thinks that Robin could have reassured John that if he came back to talk, he could do so with confidence that he, Robin, would not try to make him believe in God and join the church, that he wants him as a friend who feels free to come to him as a friend whether he believes in God or not.[59]

As we consider the conversation that took place that morning in the church parlor, we might be inclined to think that John really isn't a *straddler*. After all, he does not say to Robin that he doesn't know what to believe about God. Rather, he categorically rejects the idea that there is a God. We may view his frequent pauses as prompted, in part, by the fact that he is saying things that are heretical, and he may well be wondering how Robin will take this. In any event, this does not sound like a *straddler*, one who takes or appears to take both sides of an issue or refuses to commit himself to one side or the other.

But, as a rule, commitment is no simple matter, and John's case is no exception. He does not believe in God, yet he comes to the youth group and does so without any apparent family support or encouragement. If we knew the family situation better (as Burkhart and Oates suggest), we might even discover that members of his immediate family have actually discouraged his participation in the youth group. If so, just as he says that

---

57. Ibid., 151–52.
58. Ibid., 151.
59. Ibid., 152.

no one can make him believe in God, he may well have said to himself that no one can make him stay away from the youth group. We do not know what prompted him to begin to attend church school classes, but as his family has no apparent history of involvement with this particular church, his church school attendance and subsequent nonattendance also appear to have been his own decision. So, he is a *straddler* in the sense that he does not believe what the church teaches and represents—that there is a God who exercises governance over the world—, but he wants to participate without becoming a certified member.

There is also the fact that he would really like to sing in the choir but in order to do so, he would have to go to church. He seems to want to come to the church in the evenings for choir practice and youth group meetings but not to show up for Sunday morning services. Thus, here, too, he is a *straddler*. Unlike persons who come to the Sunday morning services and nothing else, he wants to be involved in church groups but not in the larger group that comes together to worship on Sunday morning. His embarrassing experience of failing to keep pace with the other choir members is especially telling, as it suggests that, emotionally speaking, he was dragging his feet as the other members of the choir moved forward up the aisle, as if to say that this was not the direction in which his own religious journey was heading.

Was he, as Oates suggests, rebelling against his parents, his teachers, and his church? Perhaps, but it would seem that the situation was more complex than this. After all, his parents were not members of the church and had, in fact, ceased attending any church despite the fact that the father of one of his parents had been the pastor of the Methodist church in town. It may be, therefore, that John is *straddling* between the two generations: his parents and his grandparents. John does not have much to say about his grandfather, but I can't help but wonder if he personally identifies with his grandfather in some important sense, for the one thing that John and his grandfather have in common is that their lives reflect the importance for each of the religious quest.

Another sense in which John is a *straddler* is in the fact that he is subjecting religious claims to his emerging powers of reasoning. When Robin suggests that coming to the membership class may help him to "understand some of these things," John says that it wouldn't be of any use because "they always give the same answers." Then he draws the logical inference from their explanation for why his prayers were not answered (i.e., that God didn't want it that way). If that is so, then evidently God wants a war because that is actually what is happening. He adds that the so-called proofs of God are just coincidence. This does not sound like a boy who is merely rebelling against established authority, or even a boy whose intellectual issues can be ascribed solely or even primarily to a deep sense of personal insecurity or to his having been disillusioned, disappointed, and confused by those in whom he has placed confidence. He seems, instead, to have begun to think independently, and in doing so, he has begun to recognize that the answers others give him are rather facile. It is not, as Robin suggests, that others might help him to "understand some of these things." Rather, the problem is that their answers are not very well thought through, and do not hold up well when subjected to rational ways of thinking.

Thus, if Oates is correct in his view that John has a feeling of isolation and perhaps of being misunderstood, this is not so much due to his rebellion but to the fact that he has not found anyone—at least at church—that seems to share his interest in thinking these issues out in a rational manner. Perhaps Robin was wise not to try to respond to John's "religious problems" with "intellectual answers" for it is not inconceivable that his answers would have been as facile as the answers that John had received from others when he had asked why his prayers were not answered or suggested that the proofs of God are just coincidence.

On the other hand, Robin is an intelligent person, and I can well imagine that he might express his friendship toward John not only by reassuring him that he will not try to make John believe in God and join the church, but also by telling him that he would personally enjoy sitting down with John and discussing the issues that he has raised. As we have seen, Burkhart suggests that the youth program might be planned so as to include discussions of "some of the intellectual problems which are related to John's situation," and goes on to note that John might not only be surprised to find out that others in the youth group "share his feelings and still are devoted to the church" but might also "come to new insight and new understanding." But this sounds as if John is the one whose thinking is somehow misguided or deficient. If, in fact, others in the group share his belief that there isn't any God and still are devoted to the church, he could legitimately ask them whether this is not an inconsistency because, after all, the church is an institution based on belief in God. Moreover, true friendship on Robin's part would not be based simply on the assurance that he will not try to make John believe in God and join the church but that he will engage in a genuinely intellectual discussion of the points that John has made.

This discussion could begin with John's earlier engagement in prayer, something that he did "all the time" and without anyone else knowing that he was doing so. If I were Robin, I would probably not suggest that we begin our discussion with "answers" to prayer but with why he "never prayed for anything for himself." Why was this? Does he think it is wrong to pray for oneself? In this regard, I might want to explore with him the prayer that Jesus prayed in his own behalf in the garden of Gethsemane and point out to him that everyone knows that after Jesus asked his Father to remove this cup from him, he then deferred to the will of the Father ("Nevertheless, not my will, but yours, be done"). What few readers notice is that after he deferred to the will of his Father, he pleaded some more (Luke 22:44). "I could be wrong," I might say, "but it sounds to me as if once Jesus accepted the fact that his Father's will would be done, he tried to get his Father to change his plan." In other words, Jesus did not assume that his Father's mind was already made up. Otherwise, why plead some more?

I might also suggest that when we view prayer as a contest of wills, we tend to overlook the fact that prayer is like the communication that takes place between two friends who, over a period of time, know what the other is thinking even before the other says anything. It's not that they both have to see eye-to-eye on everything, but they see the situation from one another's perspective, so whatever happens, they feel that they understand one another, and that can be more important than seeing eye-to-eye. Furthermore, as good friends develop real trust in one another, it is often the case that they think a lot alike, and the gap that seems to exist between them gets smaller and smaller. In effect, I would be picking up on Oates's suggestion that Robin become a genuine friend to John by using the friendship motif to convey a different understanding of prayer than that of a contest of two wills in which one of them will invariably be trumped by the other.[60]

The purpose of this approach would not, of course, be to get John to agree with Robin about prayer. Rather, it would be to convey to John that Robin has thought about the issues that John is raising and is interested in talking about them. There is a certain irony in the fact that John feels

60. Capps, "Praying in Our Own Behalf."

that God was unresponsive to his prayers and the fact that Robin feels that he had to control his own desire to respond to John's religious problems with intellectual answers. To be sure, it would have been a mistake for Robin to assume the role of the one who knows all the answers. On the other hand, we sense from Robin's portrayal of how John conducted the youth group meeting that John was not at all reluctant to look to Robin for direction and consultation. If he was open to Robin's direction on relatively mundane matters, would he not have been open to Robin's thoughts on more ultimate matters?

It also seems significant that John has taken interest in astronomy and that this very interest makes him think more and more that there is no God. This very interest, however, suggests that John's experience fits Gordon Allport's description of the religious quest in his concluding paragraphs of *The Individual and His Religion* on "the solitary way." As Allport writes: "From its early beginnings to the end of the road the religious quest of the individual is solitary. Though he is socially interdependent with others in a thousand ways, yet no one else is able to provide him with the faith he evolves, nor prescribe for him his pact with the cosmos . . . A man's religion is the audacious bid he makes to bind himself to creation and to the Creator. It is his ultimate attempt to enlarge and to complete his own personality by finding the supreme context in which he rightly belongs."[61]

John seems to believe that the religious sentiment and the science of astronomy are incompatible. But this is because no one has encouraged him to expand his propensity for *straddling* to the cosmos itself. Wayne Oates expresses his concern that John may be deflecting his suffering from its closer-to-home context to some larger context. But is it not also possible that the quest that he has embarked upon is leading to the largest, most supreme context that he—and we—can imagine?

On the other hand (notice how I myself *straddle* the issues that John raises), it seems noteworthy that Robin describes John as an unusually quiet boy but very cooperative and as reluctant to take any place of importance but as willing to do behind-the-scenes work. He also expresses some puzzlement as to why John was elected president of the youth group when there were others who are generally very popular and who, in fact, assume leadership in the group. John's rather hesitant manner in his conduct of the meeting lends support to this very puzzlement.

61. Allport, *The Individual and His Religion*, 141–42.

Perhaps, then, there is a connection here between Robin's perception of John and John's perception of God. For God's overt performance has left John feeling rather disillusioned, as if to say, "Whoever put this rather hapless fellow in charge?" But is it not the case that God also works behind the scenes and it takes a very perceptive person to notice what he is doing, especially if there are important others whose very visibility distracts us from observing what God is doing behind the scenes?

If there *is* such a connection between Robin's perception of John and John's perception of God, it could be useful to point this out to John and to see how he reacts. Perhaps this is the very "new insight and new understanding" that Burkhart envisions John gaining from hearing what the other youth group members have to say. For, in an important sense, they have already spoken: They chose John over other more likely candidates for the role of president of the youth group. If, as John suggests, the fact that they elected him president suggests that they must like him some, perhaps the same goes for God. Do the other kids believe in John? I doubt it. But they like him some, and that's good enough for them. Maybe a likeable God would be good enough for John as well.

5
The Stranger

WE COME FINALLY TO the fifth vulnerability to which teenage boys are subject as they begin to strike out on their own. This is the *stranger*, a person who is an outsider, newcomer, or foreigner; a person who is not known or familiar to oneself; and/or a person who is unaccustomed to some particular or specified thing.[1] I indicated in the introduction that the *stranger* is relevant to teenage boys because some boys often, and other boys occasionally, experience themselves as strangers to other teenagers, to parents, or to other adults because of changes occurring in their self-perceptions, their perspectives on the world, attitudes, and behavior. They may also experience themselves as strangers to themselves because of the emergence or development of new aspects or features of their personalities that they themselves do not understand and may seem foreign or alien to them.

I also suggested in the introduction that the vulnerabilities of the *straddler* and the *stranger* form a pair because they focus on the boy's internal sense of being somewhat or even very much at odds with himself, that is, as being unable to speak with a common voice or act with a singleness of intention or purpose. The *straddler*, as we saw in the preceding chapter, may be unsure of what he thinks or believes, or may have come to believe, at least tentatively, what he is not supposed to believe. The difficulty here is largely mental or intellectual, but it may also have important emotional determinants or consequences. The *stranger* is likely to be more concerned with emotions and feelings that are unfamiliar

---

1. Agnes, ed., *Webster's New World*, 1415.

and, because they are so, they may be disturbing or threatening. This may have mental consequences because he may think that a boy like himself should not feel this way. He may wonder what—or who—has gotten into him, and adults and other teenagers who have known him may wonder about this too.

We should not assume, however, that the feeling that one has become a *stranger* to oneself is necessarily negative (or wholly so). As we saw in the case of the *straddler,* the *straddler* may find that some issues are more complex than he or others realize, and that it is actually wise to straddle these issues and not attempt to settle them prematurely; thus, his very inability to take a position or express certainty about an issue may indicate that he is developing into a more integrated person.

In an analogous way, the *stranger* may find that there is something about the newly emergent emotions and feelings he is experiencing that he can welcome; in fact, they may be aspects of his personality that he had dismissed or rejected earlier, but which have returned and are now seeking recognition and endorsement. Thus, here, too, an especially important factor in the experience of oneself as a *stranger* is the issue of the integration of the personality. This means that the experience of oneself as a *stranger* is likely to be implicated in the formation of what Gordon W. Allport calls "the religious sentiment."[2] As he says of the religious sentiment in his concluding comments on the solitary nature of the religious quest: "It is the portion of personality that arises at the core of the life and is directed toward the infinite. It is the region of mental life that has the longest-range intentions and for this reason is capable of conferring marked integration upon personality, engendering meaning and peace in the face of the tragedy and confusion of life."[3]

I have quoted this statement at various points throughout this book, but it is now time to consider, in more detail, what he means when he says that the religious sentiment is capable of conferring marked integration upon personality. To do so, we need to take a look at his chapter titled "The Religion of Maturity."[4]

---

2. Allport, *The Individual and His Religion,* 142.
3. Ibid.
4. Ibid., 52–74.

The Attributes of the Mature Religious Sentiment

Allport begins his discussion of the mature religious sentiment by noting that maturity in any sentiment "comes about only when a growing intelligence somehow is animated by the desire that this sentiment should not suffer arrested development, but shall keep pace with the intake of relevant experience."[5] He points out that, as far as the religious sentiment is concerned, this "inner demand is absent" for many people because they find that their childhood religion has comforting value. Also, because the religious sentiment is usually regarded by others as one's own personal business, there is little outside pressure to develop a religious sentiment that keeps pace with the intake of relevant experience," so "they cling to an essentially juvenile formulation."[6] They derive various benefits from doing so: "Often they retain it to preserve pleasant associations accumulated in childhood, or because conformity to the *status quo* insures present comfort and social position. They take over the ancestral religion much as they take over the family jewels. It would be awkward to bring it into too close a relationship with science, with suffering, and with criticism."[7]

Another problem arises, however, when we criticize people for clinging to an essentially juvenile religious sentiment but then go on to claim that the mature religious sentiment is the one that "we personally are pleased to approve."[8] To say that our own views are mature and to impose them as a test of maturity on all other views is impertinent. We need, instead, some objective criteria of maturity, and Allport believes that there are essentially three such criteria or attributes. The first attribute is that the person has a variety of psychogenic interests that concern themselves with ideal objects and values beyond the range of purely physiological desire. This is "the avenue of widening interests" reflective of *the expanding self*. The second attribute is that the person has the ability to objectify himself, to be reflective and insightful about his own life, to see himself as others see him, and, at certain moments, to view the person he is in the process of becoming from a kind of cosmic perspective. A developed sense of humor is an aspect of this second

---

5. Ibid., 52.
6. Ibid.
7. Ibid.
8. Ibid., 53.

attribute. This is "the avenue of detachment and insight" reflective of *self-objectification*. The third attribute is the formation of some unifying philosophy of life, one that is not necessarily religious in type, articulated in words, or entirely complete, but which provides the direction and coherence without which any life seems fragmented and aimless. This is "the avenue of integration" reflective of *self-unification*.[9]

Having defined what he means by maturity, Allport next takes up the question, what is a sentiment? He says that a sentiment (which might also be called an interest or outlook) is the product of two central and vital functions of mental life: *motivation* and *organization*. Motivation refers to the impetus of mental life and organization to its patterning. Their interaction produces "a system of readiness, a mainspring of conduct, preparing the person for adaptive behavior whenever the appropriate stimulus or associations are presented."[10] If this system of readiness is well ingrained and fairly specific (as in driving a car), we are likely to call it a *habit*. If it represents a somewhat broader style of adapting without reference to a specific stimulus (as in politeness, aggressiveness, or timidity in conduct) we call this a *trait*. But if it represents an organization of feeling and thought directed toward some definable object of value (such as a particular person or place or a more abstract value such as beauty or justice), we call this system a *sentiment*. The central characteristic of the religious sentiment is that it has to do with what the individual considers to be of ultimate importance in his life.[11]

With these clarifications of what maturity and sentiment mean, Allport proceeds to identify the attributes that mark the mature religious sentiment off from the immature or juvenile religious sentiment. There are six attributes of a mature sentiment: It is differentiated, dynamic, directive, comprehensive, integral, and heuristic.[12] A discussion of all these attributes is beyond the scope of this book and, more specifically, of this chapter on the *stranger*. But the attribute of the *integral* is especially relevant because, as we have seen, Allport considers the mature *religious* sentiment to be "the region of mental life that has the longest-range intentions and for this reason is capable of conferring marked in-

---

9. Ibid.
10. Ibid., 55.
11. Ibid., 55.
12. Ibid., 57.

tegration upon personality, engendering meaning and peace in the face of the tragedy and confusion of life."[13]

The Integrative Attribute of the Mature Religious Sentiment

Given this view that the religious sentiment is the region of mental life that is most capable of conferring marked integration on the personality, it makes a lot of sense that Allport would begin his discussion of the "aspects of integration" with an association between psychology and the Bible. He says: "psychology's chief contribution to mental health is the concept of integration, a term less Biblical but meaning much the same as St. James' 'single-mindedness.'"[14] He is referring here to James 1:8: "A double-minded person is unstable in all his ways." He defines integration as "the forging of approximate mental unity out of discordant impulses and aspirations," and goes on to note that no one can say, "I will integrate my life," and expect to find it done. After all, integration is "a by-product of various favorable techniques of living" and, in principle, "the religious interest, being most comprehensive, is best able to serve as an integrative agent."[15]

He identifies several of these techniques of living, including humor, relaxation, and, above all, the capacity for self-objectification (the avenue of detachment and insight). He contends that the capacity for self-objectification is a point on which psychotherapy and religion agree, for both are committed to the acquisition of insight, knowledge of one's values, and a clear picture of one's assets and liabilities.

But why are humor and relaxation also conducive to the integration that the religious sentiment serves? Humor is a "favorable road to integration" because it is our "principal technique for getting rid of irrelevancies." It "disposes of much that is unpredicted, capricious, and misfit in one's life" and "may throw an otherwise intolerable situation into a new and manageable perspective."[16] To be sure, some people think that humor is antithetical to religion. They point out that the virtue of religion is sincerity and the virtue of humor is insincerity. They also note that humor says that essentially nothing really matters because the

13. Ibid., 142.
14. Ibid., 92.
15. Ibid., 92.
16. Ibid.

universe is basically comic, that, if God made it, he was certainly absent-minded. Allport argues, however, that religion and humor need not be antithetical. If one assumes, as religion does, that there is something beyond the comic, that there is a core of life that is solemn, serious, and tender,[17] plenty of room remains for joking and jesting: "To the religious person, as well as for the irreligious, the design of the universe is by no means apparent at all times, and its *non-sequiturs* . . . are fair game for laughter—so long as the ultimate direction of one's life-intention is fixed. Humor helps to integrate personality by disposing of all conflicts that do not matter."[18]

Relaxation is another road favorable to integration. Allport points out that religion qualifies as an integrative agent par excellence because it is based on the recognition that personal salvation lies in the striving to achieve, and never in mere attainment. Only the unfinished tasks are able to integrate and motivate, and that which is never quite fulfilled is best able to hold our attention, guide our efforts, and maintain our sense of personal unity (or single-mindedness): "Precisely because religious accomplishment is always incomplete, its cementing character in the personal life is therefore all the greater."[19] This is where relaxation is tremendously valuable because it enables one to accept the very fact that our achievements and accomplishments invariably fall short of completion or perfection.

Allport notes that relaxation is often impossible until one has resigned oneself to living with one's difficulty, or until he has viewed his own personal turmoil in the larger cosmic perspective. He also points out that relaxation is a lesson that is important to learn especially when a person is in his late twenties and early thirties. At this time, he is likely to discover the gap that exists between his initial aspirations and his abilities. A teenager tends to have exaggerated expectations and only later discovers that he is less capable than he had thought, that he has to be satisfied with less income, less popularity, and less ideal relationships than he had hoped for. This discovery may lead to resentment, projec-

---

17. Allport is drawing here on William James's contention in *The Varieties of Religious Experience*: "There must be something solemn, serious, and tender about any attitude which we denominate religious. If glad, it must not grin or snicker; if sad, it must not scream or curse" (38).

18. Allport, *The Individual and His Religion*, 93.

19. Ibid.

tion of blame, and profound discouragement and distress. Relaxation, together with a cosmic perspective, can play a major role in his maintenance of strong mental health when such disappointments occur.[20]

If relaxation is more likely to occur a decade or so later than the teenage years, it would seem that of the two roads favorable to integration, humor is more relevant to the teenage years. And, as Allport points out, humor can play an important role in support of the religious sentiment's integrative function because it "may throw an otherwise intolerable situation into a new and manageable perspective" and also dispose "of all conflicts that do not really matter."[21]

In short, Allport identifies three techniques of living that serve the integrative function of the religious sentiment: humor, relaxation, and the capacity for self-objectification. As noted earlier, the capacity for self-objectification, which manifests itself in detachment and insight, is the most important of the three, although the others serve this capacity in important ways. As we will see, the vulnerability of the *stranger* presents a particular challenge to the capacity for self-objectification. On the other hand, it presents an opportunity for its development. Being viewed as a *stranger* to others—friends and classmates, siblings, parents and other adults—as a result of changes that are occurring in one's self-perceptions and/or perspectives on the world may actually play a role in the development of the capacity for self-objectification. So may the experience of being a *stranger* to oneself. These experiences may challenge the teenage boy's tendency to cling to an essentially juvenile formulation of religion and help to set him on the path toward a more mature reli-

20. Ibid., 94.

21. Ibid., 92–93. One of the boys interview by William Pollack for *Real Boys' Voices* commented: "At my school, the boys don't usually have as good a sense of humor as girls." The reason, he believes, is that "the boys are trying too hard to act cool" (127). He thinks that acting cool is not necessarily a bad thing because it "can help people find out who they really are." He explains: "If you were just yourself for the rest of your life you would never find out how great it is to be yourself, but if you try to act cool for a little while and it doesn't work out, you figure out who you are. It's easier to figure out who you are if you try to be someone else for a bit. So if you act cool for a while when you're young, you can kind of try on different ways of being, and then find out who you really are. I think there are some boys my age who are really comfortable with who they are, but then there are others who don't understand that being themselves is probably the best thing" (127). These observations suggest that humor among teenage boys may depend to a certain extent on the degree to which a boy is relaxed about himself and who he is. If he does not know who he is or is still searching to find out, he may suppress his sense of humor because acting funny and acting cool are incompatible.

gious sentiment. As Allport notes, immature religion "does not entail self-objectification, but remains unreflective, failing to provide a context of meaning in which the individual can locate himself, and with perspective judge the quality of his conduct."[22] Thus, being perceived by others as a *stranger* and/or perceiving oneself as a *stranger* may play a critical role in the development of the self-objectification that is so critical to the integrative function of the religious sentiment.

Jasper: Cloud Number Nine

Jasper, a seventeen-year old boy from a small town in the South interviewed by William S. Pollack for *Real Boys' Voices*, begins his story with an account of his relationship with Hope:

> I will never forget seeing Hope for the first time. The memory still plays vividly upon my brain and heart. She was Aphrodite springing from the froth of the sea. My young, immature heart leapt, right then, straight out of my chest into the palm of her hand. Hope was new to the area and I offered my friendship. At amazing speed, she and I became close friends, then boyfriend and girlfriend. Looking back with hindsight at the night she agreed to be my girl, I laugh at how good it felt as she responded to my flirtations. That first night with her, I had gotten no sleep. I still greeted the next day with joy.[23]

Hope was true to her name. She aroused hope in Jasper and brought him joy. He continues with a rhapsodic portrayal of the day following the night she agreed to be his girl: "As I prepared for school, I do not believe that my feet tread the floor once. If anyone has ever truly floated on cloud number nine, I did that morning. I couldn't wait to get to school and walk down the hall with her, our arms interlocked. I couldn't wait to show everyone that Hope and I were together, that the beautiful new girl was taken, by me."[24]

Their relationship continued for nine months. But then one night Hope came to Jasper's home and told him that she was seeing somebody else. Jasper fell to the earth with a thud: "I was absolutely devastated. Once she had betrayed me, the relationship was over. The mere notion of

---

22. Ibid, 54.
23. Pollack, *Real Boys' Voices*, 328–29.
24. Ibid., 329.

not having her in my life crushed my spirit. I was convinced that without her, life would be nothing more than a never-ending abyss of hatred and despair, devoid of sunshine. I couldn't take the thought that my life would go back to normal, back to what it had been without her."[25]

Days went by when he didn't get up out of bed. As he explains: "Hope had been the fuel that ran my engine, and without her, I hadn't the energy, or the will, to do even the smallest tasks. Everything became futile and pointless. I didn't understand the point of taking a shower, when a day later I would only have to take another one; the same way with shaving. Why eat, when hunger would soon come again, and the whole process would have to be done over? With each day, I sank deeper into despair."[26]

No longer able to live in the "brutal real world," Jasper soon "brought marijuana and alcohol into the picture," then added speed: "Narcotics gave me power. With them, I could manipulate reality. I could travel to foreign lands. I could escape the horror that my real life had become. When I heard my mother crying in bed at night, I knew that drugs, my new best friend, were causing the tears. I felt powerful, for I knew that by using drugs, I was hurting someone as much as I had been hurt."[27]

This was a different someone, of course, but that was not the point. In fact, hurting others was random and nonspecific:

> This power to hurt became addictive. I became a masterful artisan in the craft, even as I crushed my loved ones and strangers alike. One night, around this period, I was at a party where I was so high on cocaine, marijuana, and liquor that I didn't even know my own name. Someone who I was unfamiliar with approached me and asked me for a stick of gum. Becoming enraged at his audacity—how dare he talk to me without my consent—I beat him into unconsciousness with a broomstick. I hurt him for no other reason except to inflict pain. My friends, seeing this unchecked rage burning so passionately within my bosom, became frightened and stopped coming around. I was alone.[28]

At first, being alone did not bother him, because he was too strung out to comprehend the meaning of being "alone." But as he came down

25. Ibid.
26. Ibid.
27. Ibid.
28. Ibid., 329–30.

off the high that narcotics can deliver, he went "tail-spinning into the murky, dark bowels of life, a place from which very few ever return."[29] He stumbled in the door early that morning and to his surprise his mother was still up, sitting on the couch: "The sun's rays had just begun to puncture the darkness of the eastern sky, and though hard to distinguish with merely the dim track lighting of the den as light, I could tell that her eyes were bloodshot and swollen, her cheeks puffy. Upon seeing me, she grabbed and pulled me to her bosom, squeezing me so tightly that I was convinced that I would soon enter her being. She held me there for what seemed like an eternity, crying and petting me."[30]

Then she spoke words that, he says, he "will never forget, for they made me realize just how far I had strayed from the beaten path."[31] This is what she said:

> What happened to my honor student: the tall, thin, handsome young man who loved sports, books, and his family; who considered me his best friend and always turned to me in time of need? What happened to him? What happened to the young man who, although he suffered many hardships in his life, was making amazing progress, and was in the process of transforming into a man with learning, with probity? He's gone, and I know in my heart he'll probably never come back. I blame myself, because I left you when you needed me most. Because of me, you've never been able to be a child. I'm sorry that I failed you in being a mother. With your sister, I promise that I'll do better.[32]

Her speech brought forth in him "a fount of tears; tears that had been pent up for sixteen years; tears of frustration, anger, loneliness, and fright."[33] In that moment, he says, "I realized that I had inflicted irreparable damage on my mother's psyche, and that although she had returned to me several years after her departure, I had never forgiven her and had deep down always hated her, making me no better than my father. I had let down the only person that I had striven my entire life not to let down. I could not withstand the guilt that came with being in her

29. Ibid., 330.
30. Ibid.
31. Ibid.
32. Ibid.
33. Ibid.

presence, and pushing her away, I ran to my room, slammed the door, and locked it."³⁴

Having locked himself in his own room, he looked "with tear-filled, bloodshot eyes" in the mirror:

> What I saw disgusted me. The reflection I encountered was that of a drug addict, an alcoholic, a loser. Once a well-dressed, neatly groomed person, I now resembled a madman. My face was scruffy, my hair uncouth, and my clothes dirty, ragged, and vomit stained. Stepping back to get a full look I saw a shell of my former self. My face was thin, gaunt, and jaundiced. My eyes were so deeply sunk into my skull that their colors were undistinguishable, and were underlined with deep, black pouches. I was so thin that every bone jutted from my sallow skin, as though I was merely a skeleton. I was not me any longer, and I had no idea how to get me back.³⁵

The very fact that Jasper is able to speak (or write) about this period in his life, which was evidently a year earlier, suggests that he did in fact find a way to "get me back." But he was not the same "me," for he had experienced himself as a *stranger,* and this *stranger* needed to be integrated, somehow, into his perception of himself. He was still the boy that his mother described, but he also had to come to terms with the boy he encountered that morning when he looked at himself in the mirror. This boy was somehow a part of himself and there would be no point in denying this. The very fact that he could speak (or write) so eloquently about this period in his life is itself evidence that he did not choose to deny or dismiss this reality.

It is significant that the fact he had become a *stranger* was initially pointed out to him by his mother when she asked him what had happened to the young man she had known? Her acceptance of blame for what he had become to her—a *stranger*—suggests that there was an emotional connection between her departure when he was younger and Hope's "betrayal" of him. In fact, it appears that Hope's betrayal, no matter how painful it was, enabled him to work through the emotions he had kept inside of him relating to his mother's departure and return. These, as he points out, were emotions of frustration, anger, loneliness, and fright. The suppression of these emotions had also inhibited him

---

34. Ibid.
35. Ibid., 330–31.

from forgiving his mother for having deserted him, and he now realizes that in being unable to forgive her, he was "no better than my father," who, evidently, had not been able to find it within himself to forgive her.

It also appears to be the case that he had found in Hope a means to distance himself in a healthy way from his mother's excessive need to hold him close to her, a need that was due to the fact that she felt guilty for having deserted him when he was younger. As he describes the scene when he stumbled into the house and found her sitting on the couch, she squeezed him so tightly that he was convinced that he would soon enter her very being, and she described herself as his "best friend" to whom he had always turned in time of need. It is not inconceivable that in the nine months that they were together, Hope came to realize that she could not compete with his mother for "best friend" status and decided to let his mother win the battle. It is perhaps not irrelevant that their relationship ended after "nine months," the normal interval from conception to birth; nor is it irrelevant that he says that his tears had been pent up for sixteen years, which goes all the way back to the day when he was born.

In effect, Jasper has provided a wonderful illustration of how an encounter with oneself as the *stranger* may produce a more mature capacity for self-objectification leading to a more integrated personality. For sixteen years a *stranger* had been living inside his mind and heart and this *stranger* had not been allowed to make himself known. He was treated as a foreigner, an alien, an intruder. But now he has come to light and although he made his appearance in the guise of a madman—with scruffy face, uncouth hair, and dirty, ragged, vomit stained clothes—he was in fact a savior, because he became the means whereby Jasper could become a more mature young man than the one his mother described. The honor student, the tall thin young man who loved sports, books, and his family was still there. And there is no reason to assume that he would not continue to make amazing progress and continue the process of transforming into a man with learning and probity. But there is a recognition and acceptance of his humanity that was not there before. His account begins with a reference to his "young, immature heart" leaping up at the sight of Hope, who was the very personification of Aphrodite, and it concludes with a description of himself as looking like a skeleton that was "not me any longer," and an acknowledgment of the fact that he had "no idea how to get me back."[36] He recognized the fact that he was

36. Ibid., 331.

lost, that he had "strayed from the beaten path," and would need help in finding his way back.

The Biblical Theme of the Stranger

Unlike the boys in Pollack's chapter on spirituality and renewal,[37] Jasper does not use religious language to describe his experience. In fact, his account of his experience is largely one of disillusionment. However, it would not be inappropriate for us to conclude that he is describing a personal journey that is essentially religious. For, as Allport says of the religious sentiment in the concluding paragraphs of *The Individual and His Religion*: "It is the portion of personality that arises at the core of the life and is directed toward the infinite. It is the region of mental life that has the longest-range intentions, and for this reason is capable of conferring marked integration upon personality, engendering meaning and peace in the face of the tragedy and confusion of life."[38] Jasper has recounted an experience of the tragedy and confusion of life. But, as we have seen, this account expresses his longing for the integration of his personality, and for the meaning and peace that follows from the experience of significant growth and maturation toward such integration. Of course, he cannot claim that his personality is fully integrated but, as Allport notes, integration is not ever experienced as a complete fulfillment but as an unfinished task that continues to provide motivation toward greater integration.

Jacob and the Stranger

With these cautionary notes in mind, we can fruitfully turn to the Bible and, specifically, to two relevant stories that focus on the theme of the stranger. The first is the story of Jacob's night of wrestling with a stranger (Genesis 32:22–32). Jacob was on his way to meet his brother Esau, from whom he had been estranged ever since he, with his mother's encouragement, had stolen the paternal birthright from his older brother (Genesis 27:1–45). He was worried about what would transpire when the two brothers met. Although he had sent servants ahead to tell Esau that he was sending him gifts so that he would find favor in Esau's sight,

---

37. Ibid., 86–105.
38. Allport, *The Individual and His Religion*, 142.

the messengers returned to inform him that Esau was coming to meet him and that he had four hundred men with him.

This announcement caused Jacob to be "greatly afraid and distressed," and he divided the people, flocks, herds and camels that were with him into two companies, thinking, "If Esau comes to the one company and destroys it, then the company that is left will escape" (Genesis 32:6-8). Then, he prayed to God that he would deliver him from the hand of Esau, because "I am afraid of him; he may come and kill us all, the mothers with the children" (32:11). Then true to his word, he instructed his servants to go on ahead of him with the animals that he intended to give Esau. We are told that there were two hundred female goats and twenty male goats, two hundred ewes and twenty rams, thirty camels and their colts, forty cows and ten bulls, and twenty female donkeys and ten male donkeys (32:14-15). Later he sent his two wives, two maids and eleven children ahead, so that he was left all alone.

During the night a man wrestled with him until daybreak. When the man saw that he did not prevail against Jacob, he struck him on the hip socket and Jacob's hip was put out of joint as they wrestled. (The narrator tells us that to this day the Israelites do not eat the thigh muscle on the hip socket in remembrance of Jacob's injury.) In the morning the man asked Jacob to let him go but Jacob said, "I will not let you go until you bless me" (32:26). The man asked Jacob his name and when he told him, the man said that he would be known as Israel from then on because "you have striven with God and with humans, and have prevailed" (32:27). Jacob begged him to tell him his name, but the man asked him why he wanted to know his name and, without revealing it, gave him his blessing. Jacob named the place Peniel (which means "the face of God").

As the sun rose, Jacob limped along until he saw Esau coming in the distance. Esau ran to meet him, and embraced him, and the two of them wept (Genesis 33:4). Esau asked him why he had sent the large company ahead of him and Jacob said, "To find favor with my lord." But Esau said, "I have enough, my brother; keep what you have for yourself" (33:9). Jacob insisted, assuring his brother that he, too, had enough, and Esau accepted the gift. Then Esau said, "Let us journey on our way, and I will go alongside you." Jacob said that his children were frail and would not be able to keep up and the flocks and herds were nursing so it would not be a good idea to drive them on, so he proposed that Esau would pass on ahead of him and Jacob would follow, and meet up with

Esau in the place where Esau was heading. Esau proposed that he could leave some of the people who were traveling with him behind in order to provide Jacob assistance, but Jacob said, "Why should my lord be so kind to me?" (33:15). So Esau went on ahead, and Jacob went to another place and settled there (33:17). Evidently, this was the last time that the brothers saw each other. If so, they parted peacefully.

There has been a great deal of speculation as to the identity of the stranger whom Jacob wrestled with the night before his encounter with his brother Esau. There are other stories in the Hebrew Bible that tell about the appearance of strangers and there is good reason to believe that these strangers were messengers from God (or what would later be called angels). While there is every reason to believe that the man with whom Jacob wrestled was such a messenger, it would also be reasonable to assume that, on a more psychodynamic level, Jacob was wrestling with himself and, more specifically, with his conscience. After all, he had swindled his brother of his birthright and had lived with a guilty conscience ever since. Now, he would be meeting his brother, and the very fact that he was sending his brother peace offerings in the form of animals suggests that he wanted to make things right with his brother. He was also, of course, terrified that Esau was coming to avenge the wrong that Jacob had done to him so many years ago.

If we think of the stranger in such psychodynamic terms, then we may conclude that Jacob's wrestling match with the stranger that night was an important step in the direction of personal integration. The stranger—his guilty conscience—inflicted an injury on him, thus making him pay for the wrong he had committed against his brother. But the struggle that took place that night enabled him to proceed forward with his life—to meet Esau and accept whatever fate his estranged brother planned for him. But even as the wrestling match enabled Jacob to find inner peace, so the meeting with his brother Esau led to their reconciliation. Esau assured Jacob that he had enough possessions—that his brother's treachery had not led to his living a life of destitution or poverty—and Jacob assured Esau that if he accepted Jacob's gift, he, too, would have enough to live on.[39]

---

39. In "The Galilean Sayings and the Sense of 'I,'" Erik H. Erikson provides indirect support for this psychodynamic interpretation of Jacob's encounter with the stranger with his observation that Jesus's parable of the Prodigal Son 'is so evenly constructed that we can end up only realizing that both brothers are at odds within us, too" (355).

In light of this book's focus on the religious journey, it is noteworthy that Esau initially proposed that the two brothers "journey on our way, and I will go alongside you" (Genesis 33:12). In other words, they would be traveling companions walking side by side. But Jacob insisted on going behind, claiming that his children and flocks would not be able to maintain the pace at which Esau would have wanted to journey. We can't help thinking that Jacob was also concerned that Esau would have become aware of his younger brother's limp, and may well have inquired as to how he had sustained his injury. Of greater importance, however, was the fact that the one who straggles behind the other has the freedom to change the direction in which he is traveling, knowing that the other who is out ahead may not realize that this is what he is doing until much later. In other words, their reconciliation did not require that they would become dependent on one another. What Jacob had gained, however, was the peace that came from knowing that his brother bore no ill will toward him, and that he need never again to fear that his brother may be plotting against him.

How is this biblical story relevant to the story that Jasper tells about himself? I believe that we can view the night that he stumbled home and found his mother sitting on the couch as analogous in certain ways to the night that Jacob spent wrestling with the stranger who, as I have suggested, was a part of or an aspect of himself. Jacob asked the stranger to identify himself, but the stranger ignored his request. Similarly, Jasper's mother looked at him and said, in effect, I do not recognize the young man who has just stumbled into the house; and when Jasper looked at himself in the mirror, there was a profound sense of non-recognition, and the very sight of this stranger aroused in him a desire to recover the person with whom he identified—the one he called *me*. And yet, in another sense, this *was* also himself, and his prospects for recovering the person that he had lost was in this stranger's hands. Even as Esau had suggested to Jacob that they walk alongside each other, so the two manifestations of Jasper—the one his mother described and the one he saw in the mirror—would need to walk together and relate to one another with

---

In a sense, the brother who demands his inheritance and goes off to squander it and the brother who remains faithfully at the side of his father are two selves that exist within us, and the challenge is to find a way to reduce if not eliminate entirely the conflict between them so that we may experience a greater integration of our personality (or become self-reconciled).

mutual respect and kindness. Their ability to do so would be a sign of maturity, the maturity that comes with the capacity to view oneself with detachment and insight (self-objectification).

The Stranger on the Road to Emmaus

There is another biblical story about a stranger that is relevant to Jasper's experience and, more broadly, to the lives of all teenage boys who are striking out on the journey that Allport calls "the religious quest."[40] This is the story of the stranger who joined the two men who were walking from Jerusalem to Emmaus, a seven mile journey.

The account of this story in the Gospel of Luke is prefaced by an account of several women who had gone to Jesus's tomb on the first day of the week after he was crucified (Luke 24:1–12). They had gone there to anoint his body with the spices they had prepared. But when they approached the tomb, they found that the stone in front of the tomb had been rolled away, and when they entered the body was not there. While they stood there perplexed two men appeared in dazzling apparel and said to the women, "Why do you seek the living among the dead? He is not here, but has risen." They reminded the women that he had said, when he was still in Galilee, that "the Son of Man must be handed over to sinners, be crucified, and on the third day rise again." The women went to inform the disciples, and although they thought this was an idle tale, Peter ran to the tomb, looked in, and saw the linen cloths lying there. Then he returned home, amazed at what he had seen.

That same day two men, one named Cleopas, the other unnamed, were walking from Jerusalem to Emmaus, a seven-mile journey. As they were talking about what had happened in Jerusalem, Jesus approached and walked with them, "but their eyes were kept from recognizing him" (24:16). He asked them, "What are you discussing with each other while you walk along?" They stopped walking and looked sad. Then Cleopas said, "Are you the only stranger in Jerusalem who does not know the things that have taken place there in these days?" (24:18). He said, "What things?" They replied, "The things about Jesus of Nazareth, who was a prophet mighty in deed and word before God, and all the people" (24:19).

---

40. Allport, *The Individual and His Religion*, 141–42.

They told the stranger how their chief priests and leaders had handed him over to be condemned to death and crucified and said that they had hoped that he was the one to redeem Israel. Then they added that some of the women in their group had astounded them that morning with the report that they did not find his body at the tomb and had seen a vision of angels who said that he was alive. So some of those who were with them went to the tomb and found that what the women had said was true, but they did not see Jesus himself (24:20–24).

Picking up on their comment that they had hoped he would be the one to redeem Israel, the stranger told them that they were foolish and slow of heart to believe all that the prophets had declared, that the Messiah would suffer these things and then enter into his glory (24:25–26). Beginning with Moses and all the prophets, he interpreted to them the things about himself in all the scriptures. Then, as they neared the village of Emmaus, their destination, he walked ahead "as if he were going on," but they urged him to stay with them because "it is almost evening and the day is now nearly over" (24:28–29).

So he went in to stay with them, and as they were eating together, he took some bread, blessed and divided it, and gave it to them. Then their eyes were opened and they recognized him, and he vanished from their sight. They said to each other, "Were not our hearts burning within us while he was talking to us on the road, while he was opening the scriptures to us?" (24:32). So that very hour they left Emmaus and walked seven miles back to Jerusalem and found the disciples and their companions gathered together. As they entered the room, they were informed that the Lord had risen and had appeared to Simon. Then they told the others what had happened on the road and how he had been made known to them in the breaking of the bread (24:35).

At this point Jesus stood among them and said, "Peace be with you" (24:36). They were startled and terrified and thought they were seeing a ghost; but he asked them why they were frightened and why doubts arose in their minds. He told them to look at his hands and feet and to touch him, and noted that a ghost does not have flesh and bones as they could see that he had. Despite their joy they were still finding it hard not to disbelieve, and he asked them for something to eat. They gave him a piece of broiled fish and he ate it in their presence (24:37–43).

The story of the two men on the road to Emmaus is located within the larger account of the almost unbelievable events that took place in

Jerusalem. In comparison to these events, the story of how the two men were joined by a stranger seems rather mundane, at least until they arrive at their destination and they sit down to have a meal. Even the way in which they come to realize that the stranger is Jesus himself is rather non-dramatic, especially in comparison to the story they relate to him about what happened when the women went to the tomb or the story that Luke tells about how Jesus suddenly appeared to the apostles and their company in Jerusalem. It was his rather simple act of taking the bread, blessing and breaking it, and handing it to them that caused them to realize who he really was, and then he vanished. That he was the man who had walked alongside of them for several miles dawned on them later. There was none of the drama of his self-announcement followed by perplexity and doubt that occurred in Jerusalem later that evening.

It is also worth noting that when they returned to Jerusalem and joined the others, they were presented with the story of how Peter had seen the risen Lord (even though he, like the women, had only seen the empty tomb) before they were able to tell their own story. One gets the sense that these two men were rather marginal members of the group of Jesus' followers. And, as soon as they told their story, they were upstaged by the appearance of Jesus himself and his efforts to persuade the company that he was in fact Jesus. There is something about the two travelers' delayed realization that the stranger was really Jesus that makes this story so poignant. In retrospect, their hearts were telling them something that their minds would never have imagined, were it not for the fact that their eyes were opened.

As noted, one of the two men is named—Cleopas—and the other is not. There has been a lot of speculation as to who the other man was. But because he is unnamed, this means that although he may well have been known to Jesus he is a *stranger* to us. Of course, Cleopas is also a *stranger* to us, but because we know his name, we have some basis for saying that we at least know who he is not. Thus, as far as personal identities are concerned, the one—Jesus—whom the two men took to be a *stranger* was not a stranger after all, but the unnamed man who was not a *stranger* to Jesus is a *stranger* to the reader of the story.

I suggest, therefore, that he is a person with whom a teenage boy who experiences himself as a *stranger* may identify. In fact, a boy may see himself as the two travelers on the road to Emmaus, the one he recognizes and the one he has difficulty recognizing—as Jasper might put it, the *me* and the *not me*. If so, it is important to note that the identity of Jesus was revealed to both of them at the same time and that both of them had felt the same burning in their hearts when he spoke with them along the road. There is no suggestion here that the one was more insightful than the other. On the question of Jesus' own identity, the two aspects of the self which seem, as in the case of Jasper, so antithetical, are in perfect unison. He has been the agent of the integration of the self.

When I was a senior in high school, I became interested in the sonnet form of poetry, and wrote several which somehow survived. One of these sonnets is titled "Roads to Emmaus." The plural form of the word road suggests that there are two, perhaps several roads to Emmaus.

> Roads to Emmaus
> There are means of bringing back to life besides
> squeezing reluctant breath from agéd hearts,
> other ways than dreams, rehearsing parts
> of yesterday less vigor, than tides
> circling earth at intervals—perhaps they
> but reverse intention. No, we desire
> birth not wholly new lest critics say
> we despise order. Yet the times require
> more than repetition. The sudden burst
> of tears when it occurs to us the Word
> we sought went past when we conversed
> tonight. The terror of it all
> that resurrection waited our recall,
> the wonder not the life but that we heard.

This poem is, of course, based on Luke's statement that as Jesus vanished from their sight, the two men recalled what he had said to them on the road, about how Moses and the prophets had said that the Messiah would first have to suffer these things and then enter into his glory. It suggests, however, that the two men were overcome with tears when they realized that they had not understood what they were being told and only after he had vanished from their sight did they really hear what he had said to them. What if they had not remembered what he said to them along the road to Emmaus? How fortunate that when they reached their destination they had urged him to stay with them and not continue on his journey, for it was only when they sat together for a meal and they observed how he broke the bread, blessed it and gave it to them that they realized who he was—a *stranger* no longer.

Caleb: You are Strong and Beautiful

In the chapter "Music, Art, and Writing: Boys Talk through Creativity" in William Pollack's *Real Boys Voices* there is an interview with Caleb, a sixteen-year old boy from a suburb in southern New England simply titled "Beauty."[41] It is a fitting interview with which to bring this book to a close because it beautifully illustrates the concluding paragraphs of Gordon Allport's *The Individual and His Religion*, especially his observation that the although a person "is socially interdependent with others in a thousand ways, yet no one else is able to provide him with the faith he evolves, nor prescribe for him his pact with the cosmos" and that a person's "religion is the audacious bid he makes to bind himself to creation and to the Creator," his "ultimate attempt to enlarge and to complete his own personality by finding the supreme context in which he rightly belongs."[42]

Caleb begins by noting that we fill our lives with all sorts of artificial things (soft drinks, steroids, hair spray) and yet: "We are all part of this world, and we have a connection to it. Beyond all of the problems we may have, we still have that simple connection with the world and its beauty. You can still connect yourself at one in the morning with the night. You just sit . . ."[43] Then, employing the journey motif that has informed this book, he notes:

> Everybody always has somewhere to go. I mean, you're never completely free. I don't find security, and I don't think I'm free, I've got it all. There is always going to be an occasion where you might find you have a weakness. And you improve and you get better and better. You just never can stand still. There is always more to learn. I think that the basis of things is to be as you are, and to accept other people as they are. You can be completely different from someone but have that one thing in common: that you accept each other as being independent people . . . And you might have different interests, but you share with each other and involve yourselves in each other's interests sometimes.[44]

---

41. Pollack, *Real Boys' Voices*, 372–75.
42. Allport, *The Individual and His Religion*, 142.
43. Pollack, *Real Boys' Voices*, 372.
44. Ibid., 372–73.

He goes on to tell about experiences in which he has been the beneficiary of another person's entry into his life as a temporary traveling companion:

> I've had a lot of people who follow the same surprising pattern of sort of coming and going quickly for one reason or another, like quick angel visitations to teach me one thing or another. The first one I remember was a fellow named Oscar, who was a counselor at my summer camp two years ago. He was just a brilliant guy and he was someone who really supported me, and would say, "If you want to go write, you go write, that's what you do." He helped me finish what I had started, and he was really proud of me for a lot of things. He was a very special person.[45]

Even though Oscar was about fifteen years older than Caleb "he was on my level, and we helped each other out." In fact, Caleb thinks that he helped Oscar as much as Oscar helped him: "We both had the problem of being nice guys who got beat up—you know, not tough enough to be cool. We had that in common and we could talk about those kinds of things. He was a thinking person. He was a caring person. He was open and he could really appreciate a moment. He didn't get angry at things. In fact, he was very calm, and he could always just be happy and enjoy himself."[46]

Oscar's encouragement of his interest in writing helped Caleb tremendously at school. He notes that the "big turning when people really started to respect me was when I started bringing my writing into school to show people." He goes on to explain: "They started realizing that I'm really doing something with all of that time I'm not out playing football. You have to show them what you do, you know? If the pastry boy brings in some really good doughnuts, the kids are going to like him more, or at least understand why he doesn't play soccer. They're going to say, 'Damn, he really makes a great doughnut.' And in a strange way, he'll get respect for that."[47]

He believes, therefore, that it is important to "be honest about your passions and show what they are in a candid way." If you are doing something that you are passionate about that's all that matters, and if you have

---

45. Ibid., 375.
46. Ibid., 373.
47. Ibid.

something you want to do you should do it. We should all be able to say, "This is what I really enjoy doing. This is what makes me feel good."[48]

Caleb goes on to note that besides writing he enjoys music, and notes that he has gotten respect for both. For him, music is special because of the emotions it can evoke. It doesn't require real words because "you can interpret the emotion just from the sound."[49] He views music as "a sort of safe haven" that is "empathetic to how you are feeling" and is "able to bring you solace." He mentions the group Cure and, specifically, Robert Smith, who, like Oscar, qualifies as one of those persons who have come into his life like an angel visitation to teach him one thing or another. What he has learned from Robert Smith is that one may "just proverbially spread his wings and everything will come out of him": "If you have to band together to step on someone else's hand, then you're pretty weak. You're not very strong if you can't be yourself because you're afraid. But if you can spread your wings and be independent and be yourself, you are strong and beautiful."[50]

He returns to his other passion—writing—and notes that it is hard "because you never know if something is good or if it's just a waste of time." It's really nice, though, when others encourage you and ask to read your work when it is finished. He notes that his mother encourages him but thinks that for a while she was kind of scared because of the tragic themes that were common to his work. She worried that he had a "fascination with death or something like that."[51] But

> I'm always going for beauty, and I think for some reason it's recognized more in the tragic. That's just the way it is. And it all depends on how you conclude things, and I don't really go for the clichéd happy ending. I want it to be something beautiful. The way I feel about fiction is that it is a catalytic duty at times, because it's where you can really see everything in its glory . . . It's very different in real life because it affects people, but when you do it in fiction, you're safe from that: you can watch and you can listen because you're not part of it. The same tragic story on the news would be miserable. It's when you're not connected to it that it can be beautiful to you.[52]

48. Ibid.
49. Ibid., 374.
50. Ibid..
51. Ibid.
52. Ibid, 375.

Caleb does not, however, want to be misunderstood: he is not advocating a kind of escapism. To underscore this point, he mentions one of his favorite books—*Interview with the Vampire* by Anne Rice.[53] He appreciates that the characters are "so real" and "the lesson or philosophy of the book":

> By the end of the novel, the huge significance is that Louis realizes that despite his thinking, despite all his attempts to search out and create beauty, there was never any better opportunity for him to accomplish that than in his mortal life. And he tried to explain this to the boy who's interviewing him, but the boy doesn't understand. He still insists his life is too difficult. Every day we all refuse to believe the fact that we really do have a lot of opportunities. You really can find beauty [and] you're in the perfect state to do so. Yes, you suffer the mortal coil, but along with it you have the benefit of this ability to create and to feel. It's all about really getting a connection with the world. And you can improve and you get better and better. You just never can stand still.[54]

Caleb does not say that he is describing "the religious quest," but his emphasis on beauty, connection, the "angel visitations" that he has been the beneficiary of, the ways in which tragedy enables one to see the whole of life, and the importance of gratitude—all these point to the fact that he understands himself to be engaged in the "ultimate attempt to enlarge and to complete his own personality by finding the supreme context in which he rightly belongs."[55]

It is significant, in this regard, that he refers to a novel in which the roles of the interviewer and the interviewee have been reversed: the boy interviews the man, Louis, who has reappeared in the form of a vampire, and Louis tells the boy how his mortal life was misspent. He had failed to recognize that what lay ahead of him was a world of opportunity—a cliché, perhaps, but one that Caleb is not unwilling to embrace.

---

53. Rice, *Interview with the Vampire*.
54. Pollack, *Real Boys' Voices*, 375.
55. Allport, *The Individual and His Religion*, 142.

Epilogue
Breaking Home Ties

THIS BOOK HAS FOCUSED on the teenage boy who is beginning to strike out on his own. Although we saw in some of the illustrations presented here that a parent or parents may contribute to a boy's difficulties in striking out on his own, only incidental attention has been given to the thoughts and feelings of those who are left behind. To do this subject justice would require another book. But in this brief epilogue I want at least to comment on the issue, and I can think of no better way of doing so than to draw attention to Norman Rockwell's *Breaking Home Ties*. This is an original oil painting for the September 25, 1954, cover of *The Saturday Evening Post*, a weekly magazine for which Rockwell had begun painting covers in 1916.

It was painted at a very difficult time in his life. Norman and Mary Rockwell's oldest son, Jerry, had begun to attend a Quaker boarding school in Poughkeepsie, New York, in the fall of 1945. He was fourteen years old at the time. In 1948 their second son, Tommy, now fifteen years old, joined his older brother at the boarding school. Around this time Mary began drinking heavily and was suffering from depression. She began driving every week from their home in New Arlington, Vermont, to the Austen Riggs Center in Stockbridge, Massachusetts, for psychotherapy and would frequently return by way of Poughkeepsie to visit her sons. In 1952 Rockwell also sought treatment at Austen Riggs because he had become deeply depressed himself over the fact that Mary's condition had not improved over the years. Erik Erikson, who was to become one of the most influential psychoanalysts in the latter half of the twentieth century, was assigned to be his therapist. Because Erikson

Epilogue 141

Breaking Home Ties
by
Norman Rockwell

had aspired to become an artist himself when he was in his late teens and early twenties, it was felt that the two men would be able to connect with one another. They became good friends.

By the end of 1953 Norman and Mary decided to sell their home in New Arlington and relocate in Stockbridge so that they would not need to drive back and forth to Austen Riggs Center. At this time Jerry was a student at the Boston School of Fine Arts, Tommy was a junior at Bard College, and their youngest son, Peter, was in his freshman year at Haverford College.

The next summer Rockwell painted *Breaking Home Ties*. It depicts a smartly dressed college-bound young man sitting on the running board of an old truck and waiting eagerly for the train, while his farmer father sits hunched over beside him and a collie rests its head on the boy's knee. In her biography of Rockwell, Laura Claridge notes that Rockwell "readily admitted in later years that the dispersal of his own family at this point inspired this painting, and in the same breath, he explained that he painted the dog to symbolize what the father was unable to say."[1] Rockwell was struggling "with the exits his sons were making and the scary challenge of starting life anew, in Stockbridge, with only Mary." On the other hand: "his willingness to move to Stockbridge for her treatment was a sign of his own developing awareness that he played no small part in her troubles, and he did not flinch, whatever image the American people maintained of him as patriarch of the perfect and happy family they all desired, from aggressively seeking help for her and for himself. But his own life was unfolding in ways that were far afield from any of the ideal pictures he had created for himself of what happiness looked like."[2]

The parents were having a very difficult time adjusting to the fact that their three sons were in the process of leaving home and setting off on their own life journeys.

Claridge notes that Rockwell's *Breaking Home Ties* appears indebted to a series of biblical paintings by Dean Cornwell. Rockwell had been a longtime admirer of Cornwell's paintings, both for their color tones and their composition. The gold, amber, brown, and scarlet colors of Cornwell's 1928 *Christ and the Woman at the Well* are reproduced in *Breaking Home Ties*. The seated father, hunched forward as he confronts his son's departure, appears to be modeled on Cornwell's Christ, seated at the bench. Also, even as the passersby in Cornwell's painting shift the pictorial plane to the right, so the formal weight of *Breaking Home Ties* shifts slightly to the right because of the dog's presence. Claridge believes that there was a connection between Rockwell's struggles with his son's departures and his recourse to a series of religious paintings.

One of the striking things about *Breaking Home Ties* is that the son is looking in the direction of the approaching train that will take him in the direction of the father's gaze. When he boards the train, the father and the dog will get into the truck and drive off in the opposite direction. The son will return from time to time. But the fact that he is dressed in a suit and tie, and that there are books on his suitcase tells us that he is destined for a very different life and career than that of his farmer father.

1. Claridge, *Norman Rockwell: A Life*, 400.
2. Ibid.

Also, if Rockwell—identifying with the forlorn father in the painting—has placed himself in the same position as that of Christ in the Cornwell painting of *Christ and the Woman at the Well*, then he is aware that *he* is a person in need. After all, the biblical story tells us that Jesus became tired by his journey and sat down to rest. When a woman came to draw water, he asked her to give him a drink. He was tired and thirsty. On the other hand, his request resulted in a conversation that led to the conclusion that she was the one in need and he was the one who was uniquely able to meet that need (John 4:1–30). No doubt, Rockwell identified with Jesus's weariness of the journey on which he himself had struck out many years before, and of his thirst for something more or different. At the same time, Rockwell knew that his three sons were still dependent on him. Claridge notes that he worried during late spring 1954 about how he would pay for the new house and his sons' educations: "Throughout his life, he was sure to provide his sons with financial help; though he tried to balance cushioning their load with encouraging their independence."[3]

The father in *Breaking Home Ties* would return to his farm and continue what he had been doing all those years. After all, his son would not be able to attend State University without his support. And, of course, he will not be alone when he returns to the farm: the collie, who knows he will not be boarding the train, will be *his* traveling companion.

3. Ibid, 396.

Bibliography

Agnes, Michael, editor. *Webster's New World College Dictionary.* 4th ed. Foster City, CA: IDG, 2001.
Allport, Gordon W. *The Individual and His Religion.* New York: Macmillan, 1950.
Augustine, Saint. *The Confessions of Saint Augustine.* Translated by Henry Chadwick. Oxford: Oxford University Press, 1992.
Booth, Wayne C. *A Rhetoric of Irony.* Chicago: University of Chicago Press, 1974.
Brown, Peter. *Augustine of Hippo: A Biography.* Berkeley: University of California Press, 1967.
Bunyan, John. *The Pilgrim's Progress.* New York: Washington Square, 1957.
Capps, Donald. "Charlie." *Literary Cavalcade* 9 (1957) 14–15.
———. "Praying in Our Own Behalf: Toward the Revitalization of Prayer." *Second Opinion* 19 (1993) 21–39.
Claridge, Laura P. *Norman Rockwell: A Life.* New York: Modern Library, 2003.
Cryer, Newman S., Jr., and John Monroe Vayhinger, editors. *Casebook in Pastoral Counseling.* New York: Abingdon, 1962.
Emerson, Ralph Waldo. "Self-Reliance." In *Essays and Lectures,* edited by Joel Porte, 259–82. New York: Library of America, 1983.
Emerson, Ralph Waldo. "Thoreau." In *Ralph Waldo Emerson: Selected Essays, Lectures, and Poems,* edited by Robert D. Richardson Jr., 351–70. New York: Bantam, 2007.
Erikson, Erik H. "The Galilean Sayings and the Sense of 'I.'" *The Yale Review* 70 (1981) 321–62.
Furman, Ben, and Tapani Ahola. *Solution Talk: Hosting Therapeutic Conversations.* New York: Norton, 1992.
James, William. *The Varieties of Religious Experience: A Study in Human Nature.* New York: Penguin, 1982.
Levinson, Daniel J. *The Seasons of a Man's Life.* New York: Knopf, 1978.
Lubrano, Alfred. *Limbo: Blue-Collar Roots, White-Collar Dreams.* Hoboken, NJ: Wiley, 2004.
Newman, John Henry. *Verses on Various Occasions.* New York: Longmans, Green, 1888.
Pollack, William S. *Real Boys: Rescuing Our Sons from the Myths of Boyhood.* New York: Random House, 1998.
Pollack, William S., with Todd Schuster. *Real Boys' Voices.* New York: Penguin, 2001.
Rice, Anne. *Interview with the Vampire.* New York: Knopf, 1976.
Richardson, Robert D., Jr. *Henry Thoreau: A Life of the Mind.* Berkeley: University of California Press, 1986.

Rosen, Sidney, editor. *My Voice Will Go with You: The Teaching Tales of Milton H. Erickson*. New York: Norton, 1982.

Roth, Philip. *Goodbye Columbus*. New York: Random House, 1959.

———. *Portnoy's Complaint*. New York: Random House, 1969.

Salt, Henry S. *Life of Henry David Thoreau*, edited by George Hendrick et al. Urbana: University of Illinois Press, 1993.

Sandage, Scott A. *Born Losers: A History of Failure in America*. Cambridge: Harvard University Press, 2005.

Sattelmeyer, Robert. "Thoreau and Emerson." In *The Cambridge Companion to Henry David Thoreau*, edited by Joel Myerson, 25–39. Cambridge Companions to Literature. Cambridge: Cambridge University Press, 1995.

Schweitzer, Albert. *Memoirs of Childhood and Youth*. Translated by Kurt Bergel and Alice R. Bergel. Syracuse, NY: Syracuse University Press, 1997.

———. *The Quest of the Historical Jesus: A Critical Study of Its Progress from Reimarus to Wrede*. Translated by William Montgomery. New York: Macmillan, 1968.

Scriven, Joseph M. *Hymns and Other Verses*. 1869.

Thoreau, Henry David. *"Walden" and "Civil Disobedience."* New York: Barnes & Noble Classic, 2003.

Tillich, Paul. *On the Boundary*. New York: Scribner, 1966.

Wessman, Alden E., and David F. Ricks. *Mood and Personality*. New York: Holt, Rinehart and Winston, 1966.

Index

alcohol abuse
    cases involving, 27–32, 42–53,
        123–28
Allport, Gordon W.,
    and doubts, 3
    and religious awakening, 88–91,
        102–3.
    and the religious quest, 3, 6, 65,
        114
    and the religious sentiment, 6–7,
        36, 65, 114, 117–23, 128,
        136
Aristotle, 37
Augustine, Saint
    as struggler, 37–42
    as stumbler, 15–21
close friendships, 45–46, 49

Booth, Wayne, on irony, 101–2, 105
Bunyan, John, 30–31
Burkhart, Roy A., 109–10, 112, 115

clarity, case of, 74–75
Cicero, 37–38, 41
Claridge, Laura, 142–43
Converse, Charles C., 81
Cornwell, Dean, 142–43
creativity
    case involving, 136–39.
    See also self-expression

Creator, 7–8, 14, 65, 86, 114

depression, case involving, 42–53
drugs. See substance abuse

Eitzen, David D., 58–59, 64
Emerson, Ralph Waldo
    essay on Thoreau, 70–74
    eulogy for Thoreau, 67
    and self-trust, 31
Erikson, Erik, 140–41
expulsion from school
    case involving, 21–27

friendship loss
    cases involving, 75–82, 82–86,
        123–28
Furman, Ben, 27–32, 82–84

happiness
    desire for, 41–42, 56, 62, 76, 137
humor, 18, 120–23

illegal behavior
    cases involving, 15–21, 21–27
integration
    of personality, 6, 8, 10–11, 117,
        128, 130.
    See also religious sentiment, as
        integrative

Jacob
    encounter with stranger, 128–29;
    reconciliation with Esau, 129–31
James, William, 5–6
Jesus
    and call of James and John, 60–62
    and encounter with woman at the
        well, 142–43
    as friend, 81, 86
    and parable of the Good
        Samaritan, 4
    and prayer, 113
    and road to Emmaus story,
        132–35
    as stranger, 80–81, 132–35
journey
    definitions of, 3–4
    as religious, 3, 6–8, 11–12, 26,
        63–64
    as solitary, 4–5, 6, 9, 32

learning disabilities,
    case involving, 75–81
leaving home, 2, 12, 140–43
Lubrano, Alfred, 96–97, 100–103, 105

Maves, Paul B., 23–25
mentor
    pastor as, 60–65
    William Pollack's views on, 47
mercy
    definition of, 30
Newman, John Henry, 26–27, 64

Oates, Wayne E., 109–10, 112

parental ambition
    cases involving, 15–21, 37–42,
        53–65, 96–105
parental worries
    cases involving, 15–21, 21–25,
        96–105

pastor
    as authority figure, 59–60
    as mentor, 60–65
peer group
    influence of, 17–19
Pollack, William S., 47–53, 60, 64,
    74–75, 79–80, 136
prayer, 31, 37, 70, 107, 112–13
Proverbs, Book of, 12–15

quest
    definition of, 6
    as long-range goal, 6
    religious nature of, 3, 6, 14, 65
    solitary nature of, 14, 86, 114

religious awakening, 88–89, 102–3
religious doubt
    case involving, 105–15
religious sentiment, 6–7, 11, 36,
    89–90, 117
    as integrative, 6, 11, 120–23
    mature form of, 118–23
Rice, Ann, 139
Ripley, George, 70
Rockwell, Norman, 140–43
romantic relationships
    cases involving, 42–53, 123–28
Roth, Philip, 98

Salt, Henry, 68–70
Sandage, Scott A., 67, 73
Sattelmeyer, Robert, 71
Schweitzer, Albert, 80
Scriven, Joseph M, 81
self-expression
    through music, 53, 137–38
    through writing, 51–53, 136–38
sexual development
    case involving, 15–21
siblings
    as setting standard, 44, 48, 77–79

Smith, Robert, 138
social class
    case involving, 96–105
Springsteen, Bruce, 99, 102–3
straddler
    description of, 9, 87
straggler
    description of, 9, 66
stranger
    biblical theme of, 128–35
    as counselor, 26–27
    description of, 9, 116
    oneself as, 9, 134–35
striking out
    definitions of, 7–8
struggler
    description of, 8, 35
stumbler
    description of, 8, 12, 32–33

substance abuse
    cases involving, 75–81, 123–36
suicide attempt
    case involving, 82–86

Thoreau, Henry David
    as straggler, 67–74
Tillich, Paul
    as straddler, 91–95

vocational uncertainty
    case involving, 53–65

Weiss, Reverend John, 69
wisdom
    and love of, 38, 41
    as parental guidance, 12–14
Wise, Carroll, 58–59, 64

www.ingramcontent.com/pod-product-compliance
Lightning Source LLC
Chambersburg PA
CBHW031458160426
43195CB00010BB/1018